DEDICATION

I dedicate this book to my son, Alex. I am so proud of the young man you have become. You inspire me on a daily basis and are loved beyond my ability to articulate. I believe the greatest gift a parent can instill in a child is confidence. With it, you can live an extraordinary life. Go get 'em, little buddy!

CONTENTS

ACKNOWLEDGMENTS

I feel extremely grateful to you for making the decision to read this book. With diligence, I try enthusiastically to live every day in the most positive way in order to facilitate a rare level of confidence and happiness. Hopefully, the pages that follow will transfer some of that inspiration your way.

Dad, even though you left this world way too soon, you'll always be my hero. To me you were larger than life, both physically and psychologically. I knew that you had my back and would be there in an instant if need be no matter how many miles may have been between us.

Mom, you have inspired me beyond belief. You've proven time and time again that anything can be accomplished as long as you commit to it. The love and care you've shown me since birth has been like a power source for my confidence and accomplishments. You tell me all the time how proud you are of me. Well, I couldn't be more proud of you either. Cancer didn't realize who it was messing with when it showed up on your doorstep. Keep fighting, would 'ya—I'd like to have you around for another thirty years!

To my wife, Lisa. The first time I saw you I couldn't take my eyes off you and I still can't. I was attracted to your outward beauty (which has only gotten better with age) but you have consistently shown that you are even more gorgeous on the inside with a heart of gold. Alex is lucky to have a mom like you.

I also have to thank Lisa's family, the Brunis, for accepting me as one of their own. I can't tell you how much that has meant to me over the years.

Maxine, you've been a huge part of my life since I was twelve years old. Thank you for everything you've done for me. And more importantly, thank you for showing my dad what true love really meant. In good times and in bad and in sickness and in health you were there for him. And I'll never forget that.

To my brother, Howard (Moo). I know I've never told you this but I've always appreciated the way you'd mess with me but made sure nobody else did. Sharing a bedroom with you for eighteen years got us as close as two people could possibly be. Although our physical confrontations are a thing of the past (hopefully), our verbal ones are as good as ever. Keep up the good work!

To my grandparents, Beep, Alby, and Gram. Even though you've been gone for a number of years now you'll never be forgotten. Each one of you was a character who made me feel like I was the most special person in the whole wide world. I was unbelievably fortunate to have you in the formidable stages of my life.

I've always believed that you can tell a lot about people by the friends they keep. How blessed I've been in this area.

You're my Rock of Gibraltar, 'Dosh. I'm not sure there's a person in this world who understands me more than you. Holtz, we've been through it all together, my man. From Super Bowl triumphs to losing loved ones, you've been by my side. Jimmy, we've made each other better from the way we'd compete. You've dropped the gloves on my behalf on more than one occasion. And I still can't believe that interference call! Glaze, you may be country and I'm city; you may be Christian and I'm Jewish; you may be Bengals and I'm Steelers; but you're as good a friend as anybody could ever wish for. Steve Cohen, what can I say? We helped bring each other into the mainstream. I was called too "urban" and you were too "suburban"! Thanks for always being there, homie. You're like "Old Yeller" Barry J. If there are people more loyal in this world, I've yet to meet them. And thanks again for being my designated driver the night I met Lisa! Hose and PC, you're both a part of who I am. Thank you for your friendship and for allowing my family to be involved with your families over the years. Brian Bennett has got to be the most positive man in America! And, Big D. Reid, you and I will have that strong bond until the day we die.

Thank you Jerry Salandro and Joe Sasala for being outstanding mentors. I could write a whole other book on what the two of you have taught me about leadership. Honesty and integrity should be your middle names. What a great world this would be if that could be said about everyone!

I also have to thank my Little League baseball players for allowing me to coach them and keep these competitive juices flowing. I'm sure I've learned more from them than they have from me over the years.

It's nearly impossible for me to thank all of those people who have touched my life in one way or another. Nobody ever gets to where they are going by themselves. I love you all.

Chapter One

INTRODUCTION

If you have no confidence in self, you are twice defeated in the race of life. With confidence, you have won even before you have started.

-Marcus Tullius Cicero

CONFIDENCE. IT'S ONLY EVERYTHING.

Ask an employer, a potential spouse, or any sports team to name characteristics of a great employee, life mate, or coach, and confidence will usually be at or near the top of the list. Confident people usually have a better quality of life than those with lower self-esteem - better jobs, healthier relationships, more money, and a brighter outlook on what the future holds.

Those who possess "Rare Confidence" believe they can accomplish anything they put their mind to. It's no joke that I wake up every day and think that today's the day I'm gonna hit the lottery, and I don't even play!

I guess you could say supreme optimism is a trait of a confident person. People who have faith in themselves are more able to control their emotions, thoughts, and feelings. Negativity has a very small role in their lives. Victimization—fuhgedaboudit! The self-assured are able to influence others, which sets them up nicely as leaders at home, at work, in the community, and even on the ball field. The number one consequence of having low self-esteem is that you are cheating yourself out of the life style you desire.

People lacking confidence are more apt to suffer from depression and are less trusting of others. Average or poor performance is usually the ceiling, not the floor. Show me somebody who has stayed in a bad relationship longer than they should have and I'll show you somebody who doesn't feel good about him or herself. These "Debbie Downers" are always worrying about what others think, which often can paralyze people from taking any kind of action. Step out of their comfort zone? Yeah, right! In many cases, those who lack a great feeling about themselves develop other health issues like eating disorders, anxiety attacks, and even high blood pressure.

The purpose of this book is to help you move confidently in the direction of your dreams. Anybody can live a great life with strong personal relationships and less worry about money and other stress-inducing topics. The key is to understand how to get from wherever you are today to where you want to be. Why can't you have the things you want out of life? You can, and the pages that follow will give you the tools and inspiration to make it happen.

People don't start a new job and on their first day say to themselves, "I'm gonna do a crappy job here!" No, their intentions are golden early on but what often happens is that they lose their way at some point. It's happened to all of us. It's happened to me on a number of occasions but what really transpired in these situations is that we're somehow veered off course and we take a wrong turn and end up someplace that we don't like or even recognize. What we need in these situations is a road map. Let this book serve as your road map to achieving Rare Confidence.

What's "rare" about it? Well, you often hear about how competitive the world is from trying to land that great job and then succeeding in it. Aren't there others trying to get those same things? And that gorgeous girl or that handsome guy you've had your eye on, yeah, I know, everybody's looking at them. And if you've ever swung a golf club or made a lay-up, you are well aware that millions of others can hit it farther and straighter. And I've always dreamed of being able to dunk. Yes, a ton of competition exists in this world for those that are average and even good at who they are and what they do but I've always believed that there is little competition at the top. Say what? Yeah, you heard me right.

Those who feel great about themselves and who are on top make it look easy. How? I'll tell you how. Because successful people do the things that unsuccessful people are unwilling to do. That's how!

On a grand scale, think Warren Buffett, Bill Gates, Arnold Palmer, and Michael Jordan, who worked harder than anybody even though he had unreal G-d given talent. I know you can pinpoint everyday people like this in your life too.

You picked up this book, you bought this book, and now I encourage you to invest the time and effort into finishing this book. Most people won't. Not because they didn't find it interesting or helpful, but because the numbers clearly show that most people never finish anything they start. Isn't that part of the problem?

In the pages that follow, we're going to dig much deeper into the world of confidence. What is it? Where does it come from? And how can you get more of it?

Please pay special attention to the four steps I have outlined. Anybody can put these actionable measures into practice. Be diligent about them, and I believe it's nearly impossible not to raise your self-esteem and belief system significantly.

You will be presented with ideas that will challenge you to open your mind to a whole new way of looking at yourself and the world. Unlock those chains and you'll be amazed at what you can achieve.

Many chapters will have examples you'll be able to relate to. I'll share my stories as well as those of others and provide evidence of what I'm talking about. Each chapter will finish with key takeaways that you can start using right now to achieve Rare Confidence.

Chapter Two

CONFIDENCE: BORN WITH OR LEARNED?

It is a funny thing about life; if you refuse to accept anything but the best, you very often get it.

-Somerset Maugham

What is confidence? Let's look at the definition.

Here are the top three explanations from dictionary.com:

1) Full trust and belief in the powers, trustworthiness, or reliability of a person or thing. "We have every confidence in their ability to succeed."

2) Belief in oneself or one's powers or abilities, self-confidence, self-reliance, assurance. "His lack of confidence defeated him."

3) Certitude, assurance. "He described the situation with such confidence that the audience believed him completely."

What does it really mean to have confidence?

In this chapter, you'll learn that, at its core, confidence is built on a belief system and that system is made up of you. We'll explore the learning curve and discuss that although your pre-existing conditions can give you a boost or even diminish your starting point you are on your own from there. Later in this chapter, I am going to urge you to go out and fail over and over again in order to help you gain Rare Confidence. And just taking the next step and committing to learning and growing will immediately put your confidence level on higher ground.

A LITTLE BACK STORY

Me, ever since I can remember I've been a confident guy. It has certainly helped me land some great jobs and attract and marry my beautiful wife, Lisa. It has taken me to some awesome places, like on stage next to P. Diddy at his Super Bowl XLV soiree in Dallas, and it has almost gotten me killed. That's right. My confidence almost got me exterminated.

It was back in the mid-1980s and I was a Sigma Chi at Ohio University. I had my eye on this pretty young co-ed and her boyfriend knew it. He was no ordinary boyfriend. He was a weight-lifter extraordinaire who appeared to me to be about six five and three hundred pounds. In reality, he was probably nowhere near that big but considering I was about five eight of skin and bones, he looked like King Kong.

Well, one night I happened to literally run into him. We were both at PawPurr's, my favorite college establishment, and the place was packed. It was one of those joints that in order to pass someone you both had to kind of turn sideways to get by and you would still rub up against them, which wasn't so bad if that someone was a hot Pi Phi.

To protect the innocent (me), I'll call him Rocky because that's the way he would have treated my face had it gotten to that point. So, there's Rocky walking toward me in PawPurr's and I turn to the side to get by him but he decides to square up and shoot me an elbow to the head (because my head lined up squarely with his elbow).

I turn around all mad and yell at him, "What's up with that, dude?" and he screams at me, "You wanna go outside?" and without hesitation I fired back at him, "Do you wanna go through litigation?" He turned to his friend and said "Huh?" as the whole bar cracked up.

At that moment, I felt like the muscle-head and he seemed about two feet tall. Luckily, people got in between us and I lived to tell the story another day.

WHERE DOES CONFIDENCE COME FROM?

Now that we've talked about the official meaning of the word confidence, the next question is where it comes from.

We know that with confidence you can have a great life with awesome relationships. And an abundance of confidence will allow you to attract all the money you can possibly need with terrific friendships and accomplish extraordinary feats. You can marry your dream spouse and enjoy every day to the fullest as you learn to roll with the punches and control your own destiny at the same time.

Without a high level of confidence, every day is going be a struggle. People who lack confidence often settle. They settle for lesser jobs and for lack of depth in their relationships and ultimately for less fulfilling lives.

But why? Why do some people have it and some people don't? How is it that some people can walk into a crowded restaurant and get a table right away while others wait for what seems like hours? Why can some people walk up to a complete stranger and strike up a conversation while others have trouble talking to even their closest family or friends?

WHERE I CAME FROM

Are you born with confidence? Probably not, but it certainly can be instilled in you early in life. Most of the experts believe confidence is not an inborn quality but more of a skill that can be studied and taught. I also believe this to be true but it sure doesn't hurt to have a great head start in life.

Take my parents for example. My dad was an athletic six-foot four guy who weighed about 225 pounds. He was a hardworking man with no formal education after high school.

My mother, on the other hand, went back to college as an adult. Not only did she get her bachelor's degree but she got her master's degree and has had a very successful psychotherapy practice for well over three decades.

My dad, who passed away in 2002, spent his youth on the streets of Pittsburgh's East End. Mom, on the other hand, spent her early years in rural Beckley, West Virginia. And although they later met at Pittsburgh's Peabody High School when my grandparents moved my mom and her brother into the city, they really came from two different worlds.

About the only thing they had in common was self-confidence and I couldn't be more thankful to them for instilling that belief in me, for I really don't know where I'd be today without it.

My parents loved my brother and me very much. The problem was that they fell out of love with each other and separated as I was becoming a teenager. Looking back, I wouldn't change a thing. What you see from me and everybody else in the world is a collection of life experiences that we bring to this very moment.

LOVE THEM, TEACH THEM, AND LET THEM FLY

Most parents try to give their kids the best of everything within their means: the best schools, the best clothes, a loving and caring environment in which to grow up, etc., but I firmly believe the best thing we can strive to give them is an incredible belief in themselves. Because armed with that they can do anything!

Just think of your children like a bird and for the first eighteen years of their lives you have this bird in the palm of your hands and you're doing everything you can to take care of that bird and to make sure that it grows and it eats and it learns. But when it turns eighteen you throw your hands up into the air and you hope that bird cannot just fly but soar to incredible heights. And those are the kinds of hopes and dreams that we all have for our children.

Is it easier for people to be confident who were born rich or who have been born with great looks or maybe a great physique? How about those people who were born with incredible intelligence? And we all know those who have some G-d-given talents that most of us could only wish for. Or, as in my case, were raised by two of the most confident people you will ever meet. Is it easier in these cases to be confident?

Probably, but does that mean that the rest of the world is doomed to an unsatisfying existence that's full of self-doubt and second-class citizenry? Hell, no, it doesn't! Make no mistake about it, we all have areas of our lives where we're unsure and lack that awesome feeling of knowing.

BE CAREFUL OF THAT VOICE INSIDE YOUR HEAD

So, how do you learn confidence? It's critically important to understand that lacking confidence overall or in a given area is you saying to yourself (both consciously and subconsciously), "I'm not good enough!" Very often that voice inside our heads tells us that we're lacking something. This something can be knowledge, skills, experience, etc.

You can even trick yourself if you're not careful because won't you always be lacking in one area or another? Be careful not to focus on what you don't have, because you're never gonna have it all. Having confidence in yourself is the collective work of your beliefs.

In the chapters that follow, we're going to delve into ways to learn to truly feel that we're more than smart enough, more than capable enough, and we're more than strong enough to go after whatever it is we want out of our lives with passion.

Passion plays a huge role in this discussion of confidence. If you're not passionate about who you are or what you do, why should anyone else have any belief in you? The following quote from an unknown author sums it up perfectly: "To win the game you don't have to be the most athletic or talented. To win the game you must have passion for the game; and determination and complete faith in yourself and your team."

I love sports analogies because they are so true to the real world. The winners aren't always the biggest, the fastest, the strongest, or even the smartest. No, many times the champions are those who have 100 percent faith in themselves and display it with determination and passion. Man, that's half the battle right there.

DAVID VERSUS GOLIATH

Consider the biblical story of David vs. Goliath. David was confident he could slay the giant and his passion came from his unshakable belief in his faith and in himself. Nobody gave David any chance of actually winning this battle but David.

When he informed everybody within earshot that he was going to emerge victorious they wondered, "What's he know that we don't?" They must have been just a little convinced that he knew what he was doing because nobody tried to stop him. Or maybe they just thought he was crazy. Anyway, they stood their distance and watched as it was about to unfold. And there was my man David without any body armor on at all because he didn't want to be weighed down.

You know the rest—everybody knows the rest. David had a plan and confidently whacked Goliath in the head with his slingshot. Game, set, and match. David's passion in his beliefs and confidence in himself made it easy for him to do the impossible.

An important distinction to understand here is that confidence doesn't come directly from learning, practice, or even results. These are all incredibly important steps in the process.

Confidence, however, is the by-product of the belief in yourself that is achieved through all of those activities. I can't stress that enough!

David believed that he was going to take down Goliath. "If you think you can or think you can't you're still right," as the saying goes.

As a Little League coach, I see this unfold before my very eyes all the time. A little kid comes to his first real baseball practice. He's passionate all right, as he's watched baseball with his dad and he's probably practiced in the backyard already. He's excited to be there and he's got his brand-new team hat on.

And then the coach shows him how to hold the bat correctly and where to stand and the proper way to swing. The youngster steps in the batting cage and here comes the first pitch. A swing and a miss! The next pitch. Another swing and a miss! Well, the kid is passionate about wanting to play baseball but at this point, he's not feeling really confident about any of it. He's actually unsure about all of it. When do I swing? Where do my feet go? How come I can't hit the ball, etc.? But over time, this little slugger starts to make contact with the baseball.

At first, they're usually just foul tips but they eventually become line drives. He's learning how to hit and with practice and prac-tice and more practice, the results are starting to come. And when the positive results start coming, wow! Here comes the be-lief that "not only can I do this but I'm good at it!" And it's that belief that gives him confidence.

TRAIN YOUR BRAIN TO BELIEVE

We're going to discuss this concept in much more grown-up detail later in the book. There's a whole chapter dedicated to the actions/results/beliefs circle, which is the final of the four steps. Yes, confidence is a learned attribute but you just don't learn confidence. It's all built on beliefs. The people with Rare Confidence have a belief system in place that allows them to feel great about the sum of their parts, not just individual aspects that lie within.

Is it possible to fail time and time again and yet still be an individual that has an incredible amount of self-esteem? You bet! It's not only possible but encouraged. Those who have negative thoughts about who they are rarely step out of their comfort zone to try anything new. The reason for this is they have no belief in their ability to eventually succeed. This might be a great example of what a "rut" looks like. Not a fun place to be.

But take a look at the most successful people in business and in sports. Yeah, you'll see a lot of dollar signs and wins and championships but if you look really closely, you'll also see a lot of strike-outs and some bankruptcies, too. These temporary setbacks (and that's all they are) give high achievers more fuel to succeed and that comes from their belief in themselves.

I love the following Michael Jordan quote on failure: "I've missed more than nine thousand shots in my career. I've lost almost three hundred games, and twenty-six times, I've been trusted to take the game-winning shot and missed. I've failed over and over and over again in my life and that is why I succeed." That's Rare Confidence right there and that's why he was one of the best ever!

Without great risk, there is no great reward. I'm sure you know that the definition of insanity is doing the same things over and over again while expecting a different result. Confident people, though, step outside their comfort zone over and over again. People with a poor belief system about who they are almost never do.

TAKE THAT FIRST STEP AND YOU'RE ON THE WAY

There are many ways to begin feeling more confident about yourself. The easiest way known to humankind is to just begin! After you've identified a target area for improvement, simply take the needed steps to improve. Get your learn on! Then put it into practical use.

And the really cool part is that you don't have to master your new skill to become confident at it. Just the fact that you're on your way there and have a game plan will immediately lift you up and at least start the improvement process.

How can you not start to believe when you're constantly trying to better yourself? That, my friends, is one of the not so well kept secrets of incredibly successful people. Keep in mind that anything worth achieving in life takes consistent effort. Anybody who tells you any differently is delusional, misguided, and really just full of crap.

As I mentioned in the introduction, most people will start something and never finish. Shoot, the majority of them quit before they even get out of the gate. So, you see, just by taking steps to improve and committing to see it through you've already separated yourself from the pack. Now, watch your belief system soar!

KEY TAKEAWAYS FROM THIS CHAPTER

- At its most basic definition, confidence is belief in yourself and your abilities.

- With confidence, you can achieve great things.

- Without confidence, every day can be a world-class struggle.

- Confidence is not something you're born with but many factors can give you a great head start.

- What you're lacking is a belief system.

- Confidence + passion = WOW!

- Fail, fail, and fail again.

- Just start and commit and watch your confidence grow.

Chapter Three

INTERVIEW #1: THE BLACK BELT

There comes a time in every life when you look in the mirror and go "You've got something to offer." When you're a good person who walks the talk with integrity, it's easier to claim your space. Now is the time to share what I know, make a difference, and pay it forward.

-*Tristan Truscott*

Confident people come from all walks of life. This is the first of four chapters in this book that focuses on four of the most positive and self-assured (not to mention successful) human beings that you'd ever want to meet. Their stories couldn't be more different, yet they all share some common traits as they relate to their confidence levels.

I sought these four out to interview because I knew their stories would resonate with people who are looking to elevate their level of self-esteem to new heights. Man, I'd love to get these people in a room together!

Here is the first of their stories.

THE BLACK BELT

Tristan Truscott has been practicing and teaching martial arts, meditation, mind-body fitness, and the healing arts for the past thirty years. He is the CEO of I-Grasshopper, a company he founded with his wife Sabrina, and John Assaraf from the hit movie and book "The Secret." After recovering from a crippling back injury, Tristan created programs for healing and life mastery, using ancient as well as contemporary mind-body balancing exercises. These programs have evolved into the Satori Method TM. Tristan is also co-owner of the Austin Martial Arts Academy, a center with over four hundred students, in Austin Texas.

DS: Tristan, can you tell me a little about your childhood?

TT: I grew up in England. I was very much suppressed and was not confident at all as a small child. Actually, I felt quite the opposite. When I went to school, I was nervous and scared. As a matter of fact, all of my memories from that time are in black and white. My parents split up when I was six years old and I really never had a male role model around. My mom then moved my sister and me to California. Later in life, I learned what a brave and confident act that was on her part. From that point on all of my memories are in color. But it was that shy, little, scared boy who came to America where everything was big: baseball, surfing, skating—WHOA!

DS: Do you feel that the way you were raised instilled confidence in you to do great things?

TT: Sort of through my mom's actions. But my dad was too aggressive toward my mom and that scared me. I was not prepared for life in that respect.

DS: What did you have to overcome in the confidence department to achieve the success you have had?

TT: I had to try something I was scared of. I saw people who did martial arts as strong and confident and I wanted to be like them. I finally mustered up the courage to go out and take a martial arts class.

DS: Looking back, what were some of the key elements that made you into a very confident person and allowed you to achieve so much?

TT: I felt physically very confident in my body when I got my black belt. But on the inside, I did not. I was afraid to even ask a girl out on a date. And I was a good-looking guy with muscles who surfed and all that! But I still lacked confidence. Over time, I learned that confidence is something you uncover. It's already there! Think about it. Where does the confidence of a baby come from to keep trying to walk after repeatedly falling down? I realized that my confidence was already there. But I had to get rid of the negative thoughts that said I wasn't good enough. As soon as I did that and learned to calm my mind and clear my fear, I recognized that I'm already enough. And then my inner confidence began to come out and that was "unstoppable"!

DS: What attracted you to the martial arts?

TT: I got into martial arts because my friends were doing it and I needed someone to hang out with. The funny part is that most of them eventually quit and I'm the one who stayed. It was actually kind of a fluke. You know, sometimes life puts something in front of you that doesn't make sense. But you act on it anyway and it ends up being the perfect thing for you. And when that door opens, jump through it, man!

DS: At what point did you realize that you were onto something with this martial arts stuff?

TT: My defining moment, when I transformed from a shy and scared little boy, came after I was into martial arts for about a year. The night I earned my blue belt, the instructor came up to me and said, "You're going to make a great black belt one day." Wow! I couldn't believe he said that to this petrified little kid. It made all the difference in the world. He planted that seed in me. To this day every time I have a negative thought, I think back to what he told me. That guy changed my life.

DS: Tell me a little about the parallels between martial arts and daily life.

TT: Everything that's learned in the martial arts is principle based. It's always about overcoming fear and tapping into your innate confidence and using it as a path to transform yourself. Life is filled with conflict. You get an unexpected bill that maybe you can't afford, your child gets rushed to the emergency room, etc. . . It's the same thing in martial arts. You've got a guy throwing kicks and punches at you. You learn to stay centered in your zone even when everything around you is trying to knock you out of it. Over time, you have less reactivity and more perceptivity. So, what happens in your everyday life is that you end up being more present with people and you come from your heart. You learn to be a peaceful warrior and not a warrior of violence. It relates to business as well. Every deal should be a win/win so both parties are walking away from the match learning, growing, and becoming more profitable. And the same thing goes for your relationship with your spouse.

DS: Can anyone learn this stuff?

TT: Absolutely! Martial arts is a way of life that is so much more mental than it is physical.

DS: What has provided you with confidence over the years?

TT: It's always based on experience. Just get up and do it and you'll realize how good you are rather than prejudging yourself. I recently had an opportunity to introduce Dr. Joe Vitale from "The Secret" onstage at an event. They say that people fear public speaking more than death. But with practice comes confidence and it was a really positive experience for me.

DS: What sort of things tend to knock your confidence level down a notch or two?

TT: It's always this idea that I'm not good enough or that I'm faking it or comparing myself too often to others. It's good to look at others and ask, "How can I elevate myself?" but not so good when it's all a competition. You just need to reframe to think, "I can do that."

DS: You've taught your system to thousands of people. How are you so confident that your audiences will buy into your thought process?

TT: There comes a time in every life when you look in the mirror and go, "You've got something to offer." When you're a good person who walks the talk with integrity, it's easier to claim your space. Now is the time to share what I know, make a difference, and pay it forward.

DS: You're not exactly the typical "sales" guy, but I imagine you have to sell yourself and your services to some degree to get hired by clients and students. How has confidence played a role in that regard?

TT: I've never enjoyed sales. My dad was a car salesman. I was like "C'mon man—tell the truth!" But I don't see it like that anymore. I know that every day we're selling ourselves. Every moment is an offer of something. You enjoy your vibration—your presence. And people are listening. They want to get better and if you've got something to share, a real offering and not just a bargain or a deal, then I am here to share. When you believe 100 percent that it will help the other person, it then becomes a piece of cake.

DS: What do you do consistently to keep your confidence level as high as possible?

TT: Meditation is the best tool in my toolbox. Breathing and relaxing your mind means that there's no story, no past, and no future. Then, when I open my eyes, I feel like I can do anything because I have no programming controlling me. I've got my heart right here telling me, "Let's go do something awesome today!"

DS: What does the future hold for Tristan Truscott?

TT: I envision my funeral in my mind. That may sound weird to some but it helps me stay on track. Who is there? What are they saying about me? They want to know what I did while I was here and what did I leave behind? It's a good funeral!

DS: Is there anything else you'd like to add that readers of this book would be interested to know?

TT: Everyone can be so much more than we allow ourselves to be at times. Each human being has so much potential. That's the way G-d intended it. Go bloom, man, and stop holding back!

Chapter Four

STEP #1: THE MIND, BODY, AND SOUL CONFIDENCE FOUNDATION PYRAMID

A successful person is one who can lay a firm foundation with the bricks that others throw at him or her.

-David Brinkley

Just as a house needs a strong foundation to stand the test of time and support the people that live there so too does your self-esteem. Build this foundation with great care, for it will be your springboard and your rock. With this structure in place, you are less likely to be thrown for a loop as you continue to move confidently in the direction of your dreams.

You must make a conscious effort to sustain, grow, and improve your mind, your body, and your soul on a daily basis. Go ahead right now and put it in your day planner because it's just about the most important thing you can do for yourself. This may seem like just common sense but look around; our society is lacking in that area.

Most highly successful people take care of these things subconsciously almost as if they're on autopilot. Learn from them, as this process will undoubtedly help you build a belief in yourself that is unshakable and consistent.

You're going to have challenges that arise in your life, sometimes on a daily basis, and some will be more trying than others. By anchoring these three pillars as the foundation of your belief system, you will be able to handle anything that comes your way with self-assurance and poise. "Crisis mode" will become a thing of the past and your colleagues will begin to view you as a leader regardless of what your job title says. Mind, body, and soul; all are incredibly important in building Rare Confidence.

MIND

Your brain is a muscle that needs exercise daily but not with the same nonsense over and over again. I'm talking about expanding your horizons and putting your brain on a workout plan. In addition to confidence building, this just makes sense from a professional development point of view.

Doctors have to learn new surgical techniques all the time as well as staying up to date on the ins and outs of cutting-edge medicines and how they interact with one another. You certainly wouldn't want a doctor operating on you who graduated from medical school in 1969 and hasn't learned a damn thing since then, would you?

Attorneys are the same way. They have to constantly stay on top of new laws in order to best represent their clientele. But way too many people in every profession don't immerse themselves in personal growth and development. They become like zombies going about their business as they always have and usually just getting by.

I see this all the time, most recently as the sales manager of a publicly traded advertising giant. The excuse I heard constantly was

"I just don't have the time between work and family obligations." What a bunch of bunk! How do doctors and lawyers, some of the busiest people there are, find the time? How does the cream of the crop in any given field find the time? I'll tell you how—they prioritize because it's paramount that they do so.

Talk about "successful people doing the things that unsuccessful people are unwilling to do"; this is a perfect example of that. I have mentioned that there is a ton of competition for average people but not so much competition for those at the top of their game. Those at the top are willing to do what it takes. Let's use sales as an example. If you make your living as a salesperson, and that's the way you support your family, why in the world wouldn't you do all that you can to become better at it? Doesn't your family deserve as much?

By spending as little as thirty minutes a day on expanding your horizons you may just find that you can actually be an expert on most subjects in as little as six months. There are real-life stories of single mothers who have had to take five buses to get to their three jobs to support their six kids. But by using this time wisely, after a few years of studying on the bus they became experts in their field. I'm perplexed that more people don't "get" the law of compounding information.

Focus in on two areas of personal and professional development:

1) The tried-and-true theories, systems, and philosophies that have stood the test of time and are still relevant today.

2) The cutting-edge stuff that challenges you to think outside of the box about new ways to get things done. Always try to stay ahead of the curve and keep in mind that your interests should be varied.

Don't be one dimensional. Genuinely confident people are usually very well rounded. Stay on top of current events so that you can talk intelligently to almost anyone on almost any subject. I know that the newspaper business is dying a slow death but I still read it every morning "cover to cover."

One word of caution here: Don't be a know-it-all. Cliff Clavin sure knew a lot of useless facts yet still appeared to be as insecure as a ninth grader on the first day of high school.

BODY

This is not an exercise or a "get fit" book. I'm not suggesting you go out and buy and follow the P90X exercise system although I'm pretty sure if you did you'd be in the best shape of your life in no time. What I am suggesting is that staying healthy and physically fit is every bit as important as challenging your mind to grow.

We've all heard that "your body is your temple." Truer words were never spoken. How can you feel confident when you also feel tired and lethargic? Many people refer to this as being run down. Or maybe you get that shortness of breath feeling after walking up a flight of stairs. Having muscle tightness and tension as well as feeling soft or just plain overweight are also surefire ways to bring you and your level of self-worth and belief way down. Not to mention the fact that those who are not as healthy as they should be have a harder time dealing with stress and fending off illness.

I'm certainly no Greek Adonis—that's for sure—but I do try to get my heart going every day. Consistency, not intensity, is the key here. I'm definitely not talking to those of you who are serious workout people. G-d bless you! No, I'm talking to the rest of you. Those who know you should be doing more to take care of yourselves and your bodies but have a hard time getting around to it.

Don't you owe it to yourself and your loved ones to be the best that you can be? Aren't you a role model for your kids? After all, they're paying less attention to what you say and more attention to what you do or don't do in this case.

I have a treadmill that I use for thirty minutes a day at least five times a week. In addition, I do sets of sit-ups, push-ups, and curls with light weights. I know, not the stuff of exercise legend here, but enough to keep me ahead of the curve and on top of my game. Age is only a mind-set anyway, right?

Nutrition is the other part of the body pillar. Be careful what you put in there and also how much of it you put in there. Again, I'm not a nutrition guru but common sense should rule the day here (and watch that fried stuff!). Plus, as I've already mentioned, just beginning to become healthier and making that commitment will immediately make you feel better about yourself. Again, get out your day planner because consistency here is the key.

SOUL

Lifelong learning and paying close attention to your physical being are both critical elements to achieving a high level of confidence. I believe, however, that knowing who you are at your core and what drives you is even more important.

Who are you? What's in your soul? I don't necessarily mean "soul" in a metaphysical or religious sense, but rather in a more profound and psychological essence that allows you to look into your own heart to "go as deep as you can." What motivates you to get up in the morning and to give your best to the world every day? What is it that you want out of life for you and your family? What do you have faith in?

The answers to these questions become the cornerstone of your life. They will anchor you in reality and guide you in all of your decisions, both big and small. Who are you? A parent, a teacher, a friend, a volunteer, a coach? Who are you? A nurse, a salesperson, a stockbroker, a bus driver? Who are you? A leader, a strategist, a problem solver, a healer? Dig down deep and you'll come up with quite a few answers to this all-important question.

What drives you to be the best whatever it is you come up with above? To be the best parent or spouse you can possibly be? To teach the unteachable? To take your sales to unforeseen levels? To create solutions where others see only obstacles? What do you want out of life? To retire at age fifty-five? To raise great kids who will blossom one day with great careers and families of their own? To become CEO of your present company?

Be brutally honest with yourself as you truly explore the depths of who you are to answer these questions. Then, let your daily actions be directed by those answers that have now become your guiding principles.

For example, someone who feels he is the type of father that is a role model for his children will think twice before losing the mortgage payment at the casino. I mean, c'mon, that type of behavior just isn't congruent with being a great parent.

How about an executive who has even higher career goals within her company? Well, she certainly won't pad her expense report. That's just not a quality that goes over well while trying to climb the corporate ladder.

You see, when you know who you are, when you discover what really inspires you, and when you can pinpoint what it is you really want out of life, most of your daily decisions become easier. They become your guiding principles.

More often than not it's the tiny and small daily decisions that influence the bigger picture. Align these miniature decisions and the actions with who you are deep down, who's really there in your soul, and the bigger things will usually fall into place.

Faith plays a huge role in this process for many people. I have a tremendous amount of respect for those of different denominations from all of the world's great religions. Your beliefs most certainly play a role in who you are, what drives you, and ultimately what you want to get out of life.

It is really important to balance the three pillars we just discussed—Mind, Body, and Soul—in order to construct a more powerful foundation of your belief system. Overemphasis in one area while paying little attention to another will be problematic.

There used to be an account executive on my sales team I'll call Kellen. Kellen was a good guy whom I truly liked as a person. He was not a particularly confident individual, however. You see, he had his Mind, Body, and Soul formula all out of whack.

Kellen was a workout aficionado who limited his carbohydrate intake to around 25 grams a day. He would get up at four o'clock in the morning and drive to the gym and work out with an unbelievable level of intensity. All of this while following a personal trainer's fitness program to a T.

Kellen understood everything there was to know about being in the best shape humanly possible and he most certainly looked the part. Yeah, he took care of the Body part of the equation and then some. But he paid little attention to the Mind, and the even more important, Soul, pillars.

Learn new sales techniques? Yeah, right. Who has the time for that? Study attributes of a great cold caller? No, thanks.

I would often have discussions with Kellen, asking him what's most important to him. He'd always say "being a good dad to my kids." I believe that he meant it; he just didn't align his small daily decisions with it. I'd challenge him by asking, "Doesn't providing for your family as best as you possibly can help you to be a good dad to your kids?" And then I'd add, "Then why don't you focus on the learning part (Mind) and align your mini daily decisions in regard to your actions with what you really want out of life (Soul)?" Kellen always agreed with me when we had those talks but I'm pretty sure he didn't get it. I hope you do.

KEY TAKEAWAYS FROM THIS CHAPTER

- A healthy Mind, Body, and Soul formula form the foundation for a confident individual.

- Get your learn on.

- Doctors and lawyers learn new surgical procedures and new laws all the time. Why are you any different?

- You don't need to join a gym or become a swimsuit model.

- Remember, however, that your body is your temple.

- Consistency is the key. Get that heart rate going every day!

- Understanding who you are at your core and what you want out of life will guide you through all of life's decisions.

- Take care of the little things and the big things will take care of themselves.

Chapter Five

STEP #2: YOUR POSSE OF INSPIRATION

The other thing is surrounding yourself with people that care for you. These are simple things, but they're powerful, and they've completely transformed who I am and how I perceive myself.

-Mariel Hemingway

"Posse of Inspiration": Sounds a lot like "Circle of Influence," doesn't it? It does to me and they are similar, but there is one major distinction between the two words. The #1 definition of "influence" in Dictionary.com is: "the capacity or power of persons or things to be a compelling force on or produce effects on the actions, behavior, opinion, etc. of others." Now pay attention to what that same source lists as the top definition of "inspiration": "an inspiring or animating action or influence."

You see, the key difference is that you need to focus on surrounding yourself not just with the people that are going to influence you, because that plan can go in different directions. But with people who are going to inspire you to believe you can achieve anything.

Everybody has a circle of influence whether good, bad, or indifferent. Only those who truly manage it, however, will have a positive Posse of Inspiration. Over the next several pages I'm going to discuss why it's critical for you to carefully choose who belongs in your posse. I'm going to ask you to take a look at who's in there right now. There's a good chance you never thought of it before, huh? I'll bet they didn't just magically appear, so how did they get there?

It's also important to understand how people really rub off on one another. How do you deal with the Debbie Downers in your life and, more importantly, how do you deal with negative family influences, as you can't easily get rid of them? The chapter will end with a call to action as I ask you to proactively add positive voices to your Posse of Inspiration as we examine what to look for in that person.

WHY IT'S CRITICAL TO HAVE AN OUTSTANDING POSSE OF INSPIRATION

I'm a big fan of the late Jim Rohn whose rags to riches story became the impetus of his stellar career. He used to say that "we become the combined average of the five people we associate with the most." What did he mean by that? Well, think about it. Our thoughts, our actions, our beliefs, and ultimately our results in our lives are hugely based on the relationships that we've developed with those around us, especially those that we spend the most time with and are the closest to.

The majority of people, however, never really think about who these individuals are or how they got there. If you just let it happen rather than proactively deciding who to let in your posse you're definitely not surrounding yourself with those people who can encourage, stimulate, invigorate, and trigger you to move confidently in the direction of your dreams.

Why do you think that the president of the United States has a cabinet? Do these people get there by inertia? Hell, no! They're carefully vetted and chosen for the qualities and attributes they bring to the table. Why do many large companies have a board of directors? In part, for many of the same reasons. And why do sports teams have large coaching staffs that are handpicked by management and the head coach? You guessed it, so that they surround themselves with intelligent, upbeat, and like-minded achievers.

WHO'S IN YOUR POSSE OF INSPIRATION RIGHT NOW?

I know you can see where this is headed. Stop reading this chapter immediately and write down on a piece of paper the five people in your life who currently reside in your Posse of Inspiration. I'm well aware that you didn't know such a thing even existed a few moments ago. Do it now and be brutally honest with yourself.

All right, now let's examine your list. But, before we do, remember that this is a fluid inventory of people and can and will change hundreds of time during your adult life. Look at person #1 and answer these questions, then do the same for persons #2 through #5:

- How do they feel about themselves?

- What's their outlook on life in general?

- And specifically, are they typically positive, negative, or just neutral?

- In the complexity of your relationship do they seem to be more interested in you or talking about themselves?

- Are they successful in their chosen career field with a history of upward mobility?

- How do you feel about them immediately after an encounter?

- More importantly, how do you feel about yourself after you've spent some time communicating with them?

- Are their ideas big or small?

- To them, is the glass half full or half empty?

- When was the last time that through your relationship you felt empowered to act on a plan or a desire in a positive way?

I could go on and on with these types of questions but I'm pretty sure you get the gist of it. Should the answers to these questions leave something more to be desired then let's continue.

HOW DID THESE PEOPLE GET THERE

If you haven't made conscious decisions about who to let into your Posse of Inspiration then it probably just transpired through osmosis. In other words, it just kind of happened.

Some of them are probably family members. It is true that you really don't have the ability to choose your immediate family (except your spouse, of course). There are a number of things you can do, however, to manage the power they have in relation to your self-esteem, outlook, and ambition. I'm going to talk a little more about dealing with negative family members in a moment.

What about the co-workers on your list? Unless you're the boss you probably didn't choose them either. They just kind of showed up and set up shop in your posse, didn't they? Maybe they sit in the cube next to you or maybe they make you laugh, which might be a rarity at your workplace. I'm sure some of them may be lunch buddies.

What about the friends that are in your posse? Did you choose them to be in your top five or are they there for another reason? I'm sure that for some, their physical proximity may have played a role also. Over the last few years, cell phones with cheap long distance calls, instant messaging, and Facebook have all lessened the role that geography plays in this dynamic.

Take a hard look at not only who is in your posse right now but how they got there. Fool me once shame on you, fool me twice shame on me.

THE EFFECT THAT PEOPLE IN YOUR POSSE HAVE ON YOU

These individuals have had more of an effect on you than you've ever imagined. Collectively, they have influenced the things you enjoy partaking in. Things like sports, movies, exercise, etc.

Take a close look at your tendencies, your hang-ups, and your habits and I bet you'll find the similarities to those in your Posse of Inspiration to be considerable. How healthy are you? How healthy are they? Do you eat right? Do they eat right? Do you exercise? Do those in your Posse of Inspiration exercise? Do you drink and smoke? Do they drink and smoke? Consider what their feelings are about money. How do you make it? How should you spend it? How much of it should you save?

There's a good chance that your paychecks and bank accounts have similar numbers in them also. What about your chosen field of work and your career path? Are there parallels there too? And really think about the quality of your conversations. I can't stress this enough. As Eleanor Roosevelt so eloquently put it, "Great minds discuss ideas, average minds discuss events, and small minds discuss people." Do the people in your posse talk about other people more than anything else? Red flag!

Near the top of the list of how these people rub off on you is what are your shared principles and ambitions? Are they ethical, noble, and large or corrupt, sneaky, and tiny?

The most important thing about those people in your Posse of Inspiration is how they make you feel about yourself. Are you a more confident person because of the relationship or are they bringing you down?

These are hard questions to ask yourself because, more often than not, these are people you truly care about and even love at some level. And I'm not suggesting you erase them from the story of your life. No, you just need to manage the amount of impact that they possess on your self-esteem.

DEALING WITH DEBBIE DOWNERS

Many years ago I worked on the third floor of a building in telephone sales. I'd literally make hundreds of outgoing phone calls on a daily basis. I was a smoker back then (it's been well over a decade since I kicked that nasty habit) and I would take hourly smoke breaks to go downstairs and outside the building to fire up a Marlboro Light.

On the fourth floor of our office was a collections department for the electric company. I'm not quite sure why but it seemed like there were many more women than men that worked there and I got the sense that most of them were smokers because there were so many of them outside every time I was there.

Talk about a bunch of negative people! I was astonished at the level these ladies took gloominess and pessimism to. It was like a chorus of complaints raining down with never an end in sight. "Can you believe what she said?" "Why do I have to work on Saturdays?" "So and so is such a bitch!" "I told him I don't care, just pay your bill!"

It was such a ridiculous display of how not to act at your job that it was downright comical. Yes, I found a lot of humor in it and began to actually look forward to my hourly smoke break as I would predict the theme of that day's annoyances. What a great Saturday Night Live skit that would make, huh?

If any of these types of people are in your Posse of Inspiration then you need to make some changes. That is, if you want to continue to build your belief system and accomplish great things. Later in this book we'll be discussing some common confidence killers. Rest assured that hanging out with these types of buzz kills appear prominently on the list.

Working in an environment with Debbie Downers like those mentioned above actually provides you with a great opportunity. You're probably wondering how that is. Think about it. How easy would it be to stand out to your boss when you're the only positive one there with a rosy outlook and pleasant disposition? Just go about your business and ignore the negativity and you'll quickly be seen as someone who is "above the fray." As I mentioned earlier, there's a lot of competition in this world if you're average but not so much for those on top.

DEALING WITH NEGATIVE FAMILY MEMBERS

For the most part you can choose your friends and who you decide to fraternize with in the workplace, but when it comes to your family all bets are off! This is a book about confidence, and I discussed earlier how influential and important your parents are in the self-esteem building department. It's important to recognize that, even as adults, your immediate and extended family can really help or hurt your confidence level if you let them.

Every family has negative characters among them. Some families have more than others and that can create real problems for you in the self-worth territory if you spend considerable time with them and don't stay on your toes. Here are a few things you can do to minimize the impact that these "sky is falling" types of family members have on you:

- Remember that the only control you have is over yourself and your words and actions, not those of the other person.

- Family dynamics lend themselves to potential feelings of jealousy. Just by recognizing this fact can help lessen the negative impact of the encounter.

- Keep visits short with these people whenever possible.

- Set boundaries in your head that you are not going to cross no matter what is said or done.

- Stay with neutral matters of discussion like sports, movies, and the weather and avoid at all costs controversial topics like politics.

- Make light of their negativity by asking, "So, did anything good happen?"

- Only give your point of view once, then let it go.

- If you are feeling their negativity there's a good chance they're also being judgmental. Don't be like them.

GET THE RIGHT PEOPLE IN YOUR POSSE

Now that we've identified who is currently residing in this space it's time to make some changes. Bear in mind I am not advocating throwing out the baby with the bathwater, or in this case, eliminating people from your life (although, there may be a few that deserve to be let go). No, what I'm talking about here is consciously deciding the five or so people that you need to keep the closest who will be an inspiration as you go after all that you want out of life.

Why shouldn't you be all you can be, as they say in the army? The people who will be exiting this posse don't need to be told about it, just let it happen naturally. And on the other hand, the people you are inviting in don't need to be formally invited. It's more of a recognition of who belongs in there and once you know who they are you will make a conscious effort to have them closer to you and be more involved in your life.

So, what is it that you're looking for in these people? As Tony Robbins famously teaches, "The quality of your life is a direct result of the questions you ask." Earlier in this chapter we identified the exact questions you need to be asking in regard to who you want in your Posse of Inspiration.

Answer these questions and identify who you need to silently "invite" into your posse!

KEY TAKEAWAYS FROM THIS CHAPTER

- Whether you know it or not you currently have a Posse of Inspiration.

- It's critical to your self-confidence to have constructive, progressive people very close to you.

- Be honest with yourself about who's in there right now.

- Identify how they got there so you won't make those same mistakes again.

- Whether you believe it or not, chances are you'll end up really similar to those in your posse.

- Negative people are everywhere, and they provide you with an opportunity to shine.

- Have a strategy for family members who bring you down.

- Add and subtract people to and from your posse until you've got the right mix.

Chapter Six

STEP #3: HAVE NO FEAR: DEVELOP COURAGE

Life shrinks or expands in proportion to one's courage.

-*Anais Nin, Diary, 1969*

It was an incredibly hot and humid midsummer day in 1980. I had just finished my freshman year of high school and had not yet turned fifteen years old. Like most kids around that age I was always looking to make some spending money. So, when a good friend's dad asked me if I wanted to make $100 I jumped on it. He told me he'd pick me up the next morning about 7:45 and to wear khaki pants, a polo shirt, loafers, and be ready to work. I was pumped!

He picked me up right on time and as I got into the back of his Mercedes he handed me a piece of paper and told me to memorize it quickly, as that would be my "script" for the day. He was taking me to the corner of Frankstown Avenue at Bennett Street in Homewood, one of the most dangerous and impoverished neighborhoods in the city of Pittsburgh.

My job for the day was to go door to door while pleasantly and off-the-cuff reciting the script and recording the names and addresses of those people who seemed interested. As I was getting out of the car right at 8:00 a.m., he told me that he was going to pick me up at the exact spot at noon and we would go to lunch and I could share with him how it was going.

So there I am, a skinny little white kid (so thin that my ribs stuck out), with my Mr. T starter kit on (I'm the son of a jeweler) about to go canvassing in the ghetto. Remember, this was 1980. Cell phones weren't invented yet.

I mustered up some nerve to go to my first house after walking up a dilapidated set of stairs. It was early in the morning and I was surprised that although the screen door was closed the main door to the house behind it was slightly open. It was dark inside and I couldn't see anything. I rang the doorbell. I couldn't really see her face but I could see the shadow of a very large woman wearing one of those housecoats.

She blurted out "Yeah?"

I said, "Ma'am, my name is David Shirey and I'm with the Urban Redevelopment Authority of Pittsburgh. There is now money available to get your house fixed up and Lord knows you need it."

Without hesitation and in one motion she kneed the screen door open, grabbed a shotgun, cocked it, and yelled, "Little white boy better get off my porch before I shoot you!"

I ran like hell for what must have been about two or three blocks. Huffing and puffing and out of breath with my hands on my knees, I glanced at my watch and it was only 8:03 a.m. I wasn't getting picked up for another three hours and fifty-seven minutes! Talk about fear. I was downright trembling. There I am, in the middle of the 'hood, all by myself with my gold chains, bracelet, and rings; scared out of my mind.

What was I gonna do now? It was a defining moment for this young boy. I really had only two options. I could have run to the nearest store and called my dad at his place of business to come pick me up. Or, I could get back to work. What a lesson I learned that day. I decided to check my fear at the door and walk those few blocks back to the next house. I remember telling myself, "She didn't shoot me," and "It can only get better from here!" And it did, as I ended up having three prospects by lunchtime.

FEAR PARALYZES YOU

In my mind fear is very similar to the anesthesia they give you during surgery. It renders you helpless and in most cases useless. We're all human and we all have some degree of anxiety about something. But stop for a minute and think about the things you haven't done, the goals you haven't achieved, and the date you didn't go on because you were scared to make it happen.

We all know that at the end of our days what we didn't do is what we'll probably regret the most. And make no doubt about it, fear was probably obstacle #1.

Fear of failure or losing something you cherish can be a great motivator. It can cause you to work harder as well as smarter. Sometimes fear will cause you to take actions that you were always afraid of. How's that for irony?

But more often than not, fear renders you powerless. Panic may set in. It's usually propelled by self-doubt, which is, as we know by now, at the root of people who lack confidence.

Those who fear prefer to take the easy way out. In sales we call this going after the "low-hanging fruit." It can cause you to act awkwardly in front of others as you avoid certain situations and

at its worst it will make you feel like a coward. Every person who
has ever lived has felt like this at some point in his or her life; it's
natural. But in order to live the life you dream about you need to
minimize these situations as much as possible.

WHAT'S THE WORST THING THAT COULD HAPPEN?

Had I thought about what the worst thing that could have happened was I probably would have envisioned getting shot on that
summer day in 1980 when I decided to keep ringing doorbells.
And that would have been bad—real bad. But that didn't happen.

I'd bet that in 999 out of every 1,000 situations the worst thing
that could happen doesn't involve getting shot. It usually has
something to do with rejection. Apprehension that they'll say no
or get lost or worse.

In these cases you need to ask yourself, "How bad can it be?" So,
they say no. Big deal! In business that will get you closer to a yes.
Don't go for the job because you're afraid and you won't get it.
Don't ask for the date because he or she might say no and you'll
be dateless. Don't make the cold calls, because they might hang
up on you or kick you out of their business, and you'll have no
prospects. Don't ask for the sale because you don't want to hear
the wrong answer and your commission check will suck. What's
the worst thing that could happen in all of these examples? They
said no. No harm, no foul.

WHAT'S THE BEST THING THAT COULD HAPPEN?

I'm a big fan of the expression, "A dog with a note in its mouth
can get a yes if he drops the note off enough times." Be bold! Go

after what you want out of life. Fear needs to take a backseat to you achieving your dreams. Check your fears at the door and a world of opportunities and possibilities open up to you.

It's empowering and a heck of a feeling to know that you're going after what you want and not holding yourself back. Again, it's a self-fulfilling prophecy; the more you go for it, the more you get, and the better you feel about yourself. This gives you more confidence to go for it again (and with even more vigor) the next time. It's a beautiful thing!

Take a look around at the most successful people you know. Chances are they are also some of the most fearless and confident people you know. They're the ones who stand up for themselves and their beliefs, desires, and principles. These people understand that the worst thing that could happen isn't that bad and the best thing that could happen is pretty darn good. It's really that simple.

While doing research for this book I came across some synonyms for "courage" that are awesome qualities for anyone to have. Take a look at some of these traits: audacity, backbone, daring, determination, grit, guts, nerve, spirit, spunk, and tenacity. Give me that person on my team any day!

FAKE IT 'TIL YOU MAKE IT

I'm fairly certain that I was still scared that day a rifle was pulled on me but I had to continue with my assignment. There was no other choice. So, when I went up to the next house I acted as if I had done this before and it was no big deal.

It's a technique that's been used by millions of people around the world and trust me when I tell you that it works! As a matter of fact, it works so well that it is often used as a therapeutic technique to treat people with depression.

There was a recent article in Prevention magazine titled "How You Too Can Be An Optimist." It cited research at Wake Forest University where scientists asked a group of fifty students to act like extroverts for fifteen minutes during a group discussion although they may not have felt like it. The study concluded that the more assertive and energetic the students acted, the happier they really were—BINGO!

FAST-FORWARD

Whether you know it or not, your mind does have a "fast-forward" button and in a minute I'm going to share with you how to use it.

I have a friend and former co-worker who used to be an anchorman on the evening news and he was really good at it. He actually won an award for his coverage of a horrible plane crash in Pennsylvania in the 1990s. He became petrified, however, of flying after seeing the aftermath of the disaster up close and he didn't fly for many years because of it.

The problem is that his twin boys are terrific college golfers who occasionally have tournaments in places that aren't that convenient to drive to. He used to agonize for months and months before a trip and visualize doomsday scenarios in his head. It literally kept him up at night. People who are afraid of anything do this all the time. One of the tools he learned in order to cope with his fear of flying was to fast-forward his thoughts in his head.

Here's how it works. You're scared of something and you know it. It's bothered you for quite some time and these thoughts seem to take up a huge space in your brain. You can't shake it, constantly worrying about "what if" catastrophic endings.

Now, pinpoint something somewhat related to the subject that is pleasurable or favorable to you. It doesn't even have to be directly related, just something that will trigger your mind to the more positive thoughts the minute your fear creeps in. In my buddy's case, he would fast-forward his mind to the golf course and watching his boys have the time of their lives playing the game they love. It's a confident and progressive technique that can help you overcome almost any fear. The important part is to plan ahead to what and where that place is in your head that you're going to hit the fast-forward button to.

KEY TAKEAWAYS FROM THIS CHAPTER

- Fear paralyzes you.

- When it strikes consider what the worst thing is that could happen.

- Then, think about the best thing that could happen if the fear was brushed aside.

- Act "as if."

- The fast-forward technique will always take you to a better place.

Chapter Seven

STEP #4: UNDERSTANDING THE ACTIONS—RESULTS—BELIEFS CIRCLE

Action is a great restorer and builder of confidence. Inaction is not only the result, but the cause, of fear. Perhaps the action you take will be successful; perhaps different action or adjustments will have to follow. But any action is better than no action at all.

-Norman Vincent Peale

We've all been in this situation. We know what we have to do to get where we want to go. The problem is that we don't always believe in either ourselves, the process, or that we'll achieve the expected outcome. As mentioned earlier this feeling of doubt can be paralyzing. Paralyzing to your psyche and paralyzing to your ability to act. And because of it your results suffer.

Step #4 of this process is your understanding and implementation of the ACTIONS—RESULTS—BELIEFS CIRCLE. This is the step that not only forces you to ACT and ACT NOW, but will lead to something much greater; BELIEFS! Remember, your belief system about yourself is at the core of everything you do and how well you do it.

SUCCESS FORMULA DEFINED

In order to help you understand this ACTION—RESULTS—BELIEF CIRCLE a little bit better let's take a quick look at the simplest formula for success I've ever seen:

<u>COMPETENCE + FREQUENCY = SUCCESS</u>

COMPETENCE: You better be darn good at what you do and you get there by continuing to upgrade your skills through constant learning and practice.

FREQUENCY: You have to do it a lot! Stop looking for short-cuts and man up (or woman up—whatever the case may be). It's called elbow grease!

SUCCESS: The eventual sum of COMPETENCE and FREQUENCY.

It's not rocket science but it is extremely powerful in its simplicity. It's like John Wooden, UCLA's legendary basketball coach, used to preach. You don't have to do a million things to be successful. Do a few and do them to the best of your ability and do them over and over and over again. And, eventually, you'll be the absolute best that you can be.

ACTIONS

Even when you don't feel as confident as you should—about something that you know you've got to do—you must ACT!

You've got the knowledge (the MIND part of Step #1). You're feeling strong and healthy (the BODY part of Step #1). And you know you've got to do it because it's imperative to help you in taking care of what's most important to you (the SOUL part of Step #1).

By now you have a "Posse of Inspiration" (Step #2) that will move, stir, excite, and spark you to do the things you never thought possible. They are an incredible support system for you, as they've been there before!

Muster up that courage that we discussed in the last chapter (Step #3) and ACT NOW! And then ACT again, and again, and again. Nobody is great at whatever they're doing the first few times they do it. It takes time. But there's got to be a jump-off point and this is yours. Don't think about it for too long as you may talk yourself out of it. As Nike advocates, JUST DO IT!

RESULTS

Eventually the RESULTS will come. How long they will take and to what degree are entirely up to you. Much of it has to do with your skill level and the degree of persistence and commitment you are willing to demonstrate. But the results will come if you're doing all the right things and doing them often enough.

Keep in mind that without ACTING the chances of having RESULTS are zero, nada, nothing. . .also known as having diddly-squat! Don't be one of those people that talks a good game and never has anything to show for it. RESULTS speak for themselves. And even tiny ones can propel you like a rocket into the future!

Soon enough, the compilation of your RESULTS will begin to grow. And grow. And grow. This is when you want to step on the proverbial gas pedal and collect as many of them as you possibly can. After all, these victories are the fruits of your labor, your compensation for a job well done. Your triumphs, both big and small, will begin to perpetuate themselves. Which brings us to the best part. . .

BELIEFS

Now you BELIEVE! You acted out of courage when you were scared. You kept at it during the rough stages when it wasn't working as well as you had wished. You started seeing some minuscule results. And then they grew, and grew, and grew. And now you BELIEVE in what you're doing—what a beautiful thing!

Once you BELIEVE, man, the sky is the limit! It's all there for the taking. I've felt it myself and you will too. Sometimes it comes over you in waves of confidence and feelings of I CAN DO ANYTHING! WOW! That's what I'm talking about right there! Put that feeling in a bottle and exult in the possibilities that now exist for you. That's how you achieve Rare Confidence.

The belief part can't happen until you first ACT and then begin to see RESULTS. It would be nice if we all could just believe from the get-go but that's not the way of the world. It has to come from inside you and there has to be tangible evidence in order for you to get on board.

ACTIONS + RESULTS + BELIEFS = **POWERFUL STUFF**

SCENARIOS

Let's look at some examples as to how this works in real life.

Think of the guy who is too scared to ask anybody out on a date. Forget about the beautiful girls, he won't even approach the homely ones! But what if he gathers up all of his courage and finally acts by asking out a girl that even he thinks he has a reasonable shot at, based on his self-limiting beliefs. And guess what—she says yes! And they have a great time. Next my man starts to ask prettier girls out and they say yes too! Before you know it, he feels like Hugh Hefner, and he decides who he wants to date. That's Rare Confidence.

I used to hate to fly; scared to death of it, actually. I'd do all I could to avoid it. I'd drive when possible or arrange meetings by phone instead. But this was really getting in the way of doing the things I needed to do and becoming the person I wanted to be. So I said, "The hell with it—let's fly." And in that one year alone I flew during forty-five of those weeks. I ACTED. And guess what? I got where I needed to go quickly and without any drama (which is what I was fearful of). And my job performance rose and the company took notice and promoted me. RESULTS! And before long I was jumping on and off airplanes with the same carefree attitude that most people exhibit when they get in and out of the shower.

A great golfer I'm not. Every swing used to be an experiment. Consistency in my mechanics was a foreign concept.

A good friend who also happens to be a strong golfer helped me with my swing. He corrected some blatant errors I was making and showed me how to minimize my slice and get more distance off the tee. At first, I felt like someone who was deformed by the way I was now told to hold the club and then swing it. It was so unnatural. I hated it. My golfing buddy, however, implored me to stick with it. And I did, over and over and over again. I ACTED. And the RESULTS finally started to show! I BELIEVE I can go out there and enjoy eighteen holes without embarrassing myself! Now I'm no Phil Mickelson (and never will be!) but at least now I look forward to outings rather than dread them.

Consider the salesperson that is afraid to go after new business. It's pretty difficult to make a living in the sales profession if you're not adept at this part of the game. Cold calling, after all, is the lifeblood of the industry. Those who do it well and often are usually the ones with greater job security and larger commission checks. Those who do it rarely and poorly typically jump from job to job and have a real struggle just getting by most of the time.

Well, this salesperson finally makes a commitment to begin prospecting and cold calling on a regular basis. At first, he sounds like a rambling fool. It happens. He has to fight though this. But he leans on what he has learned about how to make a cold call the proper way. He feels fit and strong because he's taking care of his body. And he knows he has to make these calls because it will help him make more sales and get promoted. And that will help him take care of his family better, which is the most important thing to who he is deep down in his soul.

He has surrounded himself with the best salespeople he knows, both in and out of his company. After summoning all of his courage, he continues to reach out to potential buyers. Before you know it, he begins to secure sales appointments, one after another after another. And then, some of those appointments start to turn into small sales and then medium sales and then larger sales. Finally, the fruits of his labor emerge. What a belief system he has now! There's no more wishing and hoping for a miracle to happen. This guy knows it's going to happen because he's been there and done that. That's what the ACTIONS—RESULTS—BELIEFS CIRCLE is all about.

You can't wait until you believe to ACT. It will never happen. Don't wait for results either. They will never come without ACTION. Hope is not a strategy. ACTION is. There's an old saying that goes, "Hope in one hand and shit in the other and see which one fills up faster." Sorry for the graphic detail, but you get the idea. Do something. Anything to get you out of the place you are now and headed in the direction you want to be going.

KEY TAKEAWAYS FROM THIS CHAPTER

- ACTIONS come before RESULTS.

- Utilize the simple Success Formula to help you achieve the desired RESULTS. RESULTS come before BELIEFS.

- There are no shortcuts to achieving BELIEFS, but when built the proper way, they will stand the test of time.

- BELIEFS are at the core of your confidence level.

Chapter Eight

WHAT WE CAN LEARN FROM THE SPORTS WORLD

"I'm not old enough to play baseball or football. I'm not eight yet. My mom told me when you start baseball, you aren't going to be able to run that fast because you had an operation. I told Mom I wouldn't need to run that fast. When I play baseball, I'll just hit them out of the park. Then I'll be able to walk."

-Edward J. McGrath, Jr., An Exceptional View of Life, quoted in Chicken Soup for the Soul by Jack Canfield and Mark Victor Hansen, 1993

The Pittsburgh Steelers, the New York Yankees, the Los Angeles Lakers, Duke Basketball—just the mention of any of these outstanding organizations brings raw emotions for sports fans all over the world. You either love 'em or you hate 'em but just say their names and a few distinct qualities come to mind immediately: winning, success, championships, and pride. These are confident organizations from the front offices, to the coaching staffs, to the players and their massive fan bases. They always have a tremendous expectation of accomplishment.

Every great organization that consistently wins has a few characteristics in common just as confident people do. Things like process, consistency, and belief (there's that word again) come quickly to mind.

In this chapter, I'm going to talk about the world of sports. More specifically, what we can learn from it in terms of confidence. We'll explore examples of athletes who may have lacked some in the talent or physical attributes department but have prospered due to their belief in themselves. We'll also take a look at a few big-time players who lost it. No, they didn't lose their size or their speed; they lost that inner feeling that they could compete at the highest level and get it done.

This chapter wouldn't be complete if boxing wasn't touched upon, as it's the ultimate "mano-a-mano" competition where confidence is, again, everything. And what happens when losing franchises resort to gimmicks to get people to their games once their fans have lost all confidence in them. Hint—it doesn't work in real life either.

WHY NOT US?

Just like with people, teams that have a strong belief in themselves can do amazing things. I'm talking about above and beyond what others gave them a chance to do. Just tune in to any first-round NCAA tournament hoop game on that first Thursday or Friday in mid-March and you'll see what I mean. Every year there are big-time upsets. Teams from the so-called mid-major conferences shock the world by beating one of college basketball's traditional power brokers. Take a closer look and what you'll see is a team that gains a stronger belief in itself as the game continues. You can literally see their confidence growing right before your very eyes.

I've got to give a special shout-out here to those resilient Butler Bulldogs, a perfect example of this, who made two straight NCAA championship games coming out of the Horizon League.

Often, these teams will adopt the rallying cry, "Why not us?" They're basically saying, "Hey, we can do this too." Or, "Don't we deserve to be right there with the best?" Well, you as an individual have to develop that same mind-set in order to achieve the level of confidence that will help you reach your dreams.

PROCESS

Over the years, those who detest my beloved Pittsburgh Steelers have called them many things. Things like cheap, old-fashioned, and no-frills. I always tell people that once you're done calling them all of that nonsense make sure to also call them six-time Super Bowl champions! That's the most in NFL history, by the way.

How did they do this? How did the Steelers become the most dominant franchise in professional football over the last forty years? The simple answer is that they have a great process. The Steelers have fine-tuned their process for winning down to a science. They have won Super Bowls during years in which they had numerous significant injuries to key players yet they just plug in a relative unknown who usually seems to step up and get the job done. As Coach Mike Tomlin often says, "The level of expectation doesn't change." Just as in real life, with a great process, ordinary people can do extraordinary things.

The Steelers have proven repeatedly what can be accomplished when the focal point is the process. For example, the Steelers have run a 3-4 defense for almost thirty years now. They'll draft undersized defensive ends and convert them into speed rushing outside linebackers. They always strive to be a physical bunch on both sides of the football. They never overpay for a free agent, whether it be their own player or otherwise, and they give back to their community as well as any other team in professional sports.

Trust me when I tell you that it's the exact same way in business and in life. How do you think McDonald's is able to put a franchise anywhere in the world where there is a population base and succeed? It's all about the process. Show me a great salesperson and I'll show you somebody who never wings it and is always prepared; somebody who is constantly filling his or her pipeline while at the same time moving other opportunities forward or moving them out; someone who never complains about the sale that got away but, instead, adopts the Doritos mind-set of "we'll make more."

CONSISTENCY

The New York Yankees have won twenty-seven World Series championships. As of this writing, the Bronx bombers have appeared in forty of the hundred and five World Series classics ever played. That's what I call consistency! Those numbers reiterate what was said earlier; there's a lot of competition in this world when you're average, but not so much when you're on top. The Yankees' level of consistency since they won their first World Series in 1923 has been nothing short of remarkable and really the stuff of legend.

Consider the fact that the men in pinstripes have won multiple World Series in every decade since with the lone exception of the 1980s when they didn't win any. Next to the word consistency in the dictionary should be that iconic NY logo that the Yankees wear so proudly on their caps (sorry, Red Sox fans, but those are the facts and you've got seven titles of your own anyway).

Consistency and confidence work hand in hand. As consistently good as they've been over the last eighty years, they're confident that their younger players, for whom they've paid top dollar on the free agent market, will step in and not only fill a void but improve upon it.

Doing the right things consistently breeds success. It doesn't happen overnight. Try doing curls with your right arm and do three sets of fifteen every day with a dumbbell. After one day— nothing. After one week—still not much. After one month—hey, look at that. After one year, wow!

Too many people give up or change what they're doing too often. I know I said earlier that the definition of insanity is doing the same thing repeatedly and expecting a different result. Well, that famous saying addresses doing the wrong things. The right things are usually somewhat more difficult to do and require more effort, which explains why it is so hard for most people to stick with it. Doing the right things consistently, even when you don't feel like it, will undoubtedly pay off in the long run. You think the Yankees believe that?

BELIEF

Do you believe in miracles? Yes! In the introduction I wrote that those who possess Rare Confidence believe they can accomplish anything they put their mind to. Never was this more evident than in the Lake Placid Olympics in 1980 when a group of American college kids defeated essentially what was the greatest professional hockey team in the world, the Soviets, and subsequently went on to win the gold medal. To say this one game was a victory of epic proportions would be an understatement.

This game was more than about hockey. To those in the United States it was good versus evil. The problem was that the good had what appeared to be no chance for success, except that the American kids didn't know that. It was at the height of the Cold War and the Soviet Union had just invaded Afghanistan. President Jimmy Carter was openly discussing America's eventual boycott of the 1980 Summer Olympics later that year in Moscow in protest of the invasion. Most people in the world at that time believed the Americans and the Soviets had nuclear weapons pointed at each other and ready to be launched at a moment's notice. This was no ordinary hockey game!

How could the American kids even compete? The odds were not in their favor and it wasn't even close. They were college kids essentially playing together for the first time against a Soviet team that had legendary players, three of whom would eventually be inducted into the Hockey Hall of Fame. One of those three was Vladislav Tretiak, widely considered the best goaltender in the world. To make things seem even worse, the Soviets had destroyed the young American team 10-3 less than two weeks earlier in Madison Square Garden in New York in the last exhibition game leading up to the Olympics. The Soviets had won the gold medal in every Winter Olympics leading up to 1980, dating all the way back to 1964.

The deck was stacked against the Americans but the United States head coach, Herb Brooks, believed. He believed in his system, he believed in his players, he believed in their preparation, and he believed in his game plan. And his group of college kids believed that they could out-finesse and out-instigate the older and slower Soviets.

Before the contest, Coach Brooks gave one of the all-time great pregame speeches, immortalized in the 2004 movie Miracle. The United States team went to the first intermission tied at 2, but then trailed 3-2 after two periods had been played. Mark

Johnson, however, scored at the end of a power play about eight and a half minutes into the third period, tying the score. And when team captain Mike Eruzione scored from the high slot with ten minutes to go to give the United States the lead, everybody in the building believed they were watching history unfold.

The Americans withstood furious rally after rally by the Soviets. ABC television's Al Michaels ended the game with one of the greatest sports calls in TV history: "Eleven seconds, you've got ten seconds, the countdown going on right now. Morrow up to Silk. Five seconds left in the game. Do you believe in miracles? Yes!"

What many people don't remember is that the United States still had to beat Finland a few days later to win the gold medal, which they again did in comeback fashion.

THE LITTLE DUNKER

Never underestimate what belief can do for your confidence and what that confidence can do for the results in your life. Spud Webb is a perfect example of this.

Spud was a fourth-round pick in the 1985 NBA Draft by the Atlanta Hawks. He was the shortest player in the league at that time at only five seven. Spud never let his height or lack thereof limit his belief in himself or what he could or couldn't do on the basketball court. He ended up playing twelve years in the NBA while scoring over eight thousand points and recording 4,342 assists but none of that is what he's remembered for.

No, it was in the 1986 NBA Slam Dunk Contest where Spud etched his lure. Few who witnessed it would ever forget what the little man did that night. Most wondered why he was even entered into the contest, including fellow dunker and Atlanta Hawk teammate Dominique Wilkins, who was the defending slam dunk champion from the previous year.

Nobody, and I mean nobody, believed that a five seven guy should even be in the NBA Slam Dunk Contest much less have any chance to win it. Nobody believed except for Spud, and his confidence soared as he orchestrated some of the best moves in slam dunk contest history. With his elevator two-handed double pump dunk, his 360-degree helicopter throwdown, a 180-degree reverse double pump slam, and his reverse two-handed strawberry jam from a bounce off the floor just to name a few.

Spud walked away that night with the golden ball trophy as the winner of the 1986 NBA Slam Dunk Contest. With it, he gave short guys everywhere the confidence to hoop with the big boys. As Spud proved, you're really only limited by your beliefs. The belief in yourself and the limitations your mind says you can or cannot accomplish.

HOW'S THIS FOR RARE CONFIDENCE

Although not sports related, I felt this next tidbit of confidence was appropriate for this chapter. The United States military, more specifically the highly trained Navy Seals Team 6, have finally tracked down and killed Osama bin Laden. These dudes are the baddest of the bad. If I were ever in an alley fight, I'd sure want them on my side.

As you know, it was the biggest news story in the world for quite a while. I was watching CNN the night this all unfolded and the subject of torture, specifically waterboarding, was being debated between host Piers Morgan and Rep. Peter King of New York.

Information had come out that these sorts of interrogation techniques were utilized a number of years ago and it eventually led us to Osama bin Laden. The United States government has since outlawed these procedures but Representative King mentioned that we should revisit the use of them. Piers Morgan asked Representative King, "Well, what if one of our Navy Seals was captured and was subsequently waterboarded? How would you feel about that?" Representative King answered, "They've already been waterboarded as part of their training. They're ready for anything." Now that's Rare Confidence!

CONFIDENCE LOST IS HARD TO WATCH

It's not a pretty thing to see when athletes lose their confidence. Think about it. You may be feeling less than stellar about something at work but hundreds of thousands or even millions of people aren't watching you live in person and on television. Chuck Knoblauch and Steve Blass come immediately to mind.

Although they played in different eras, Blass from 1964-1975 and Knoblauch from 1991-2002, they shared a similar ending to their baseball careers. They both lost confidence in their ability to throw the baseball with any accuracy, which is kind of important for a baseball player. This affliction has since been coined "Steve Blass disease" and is one of the worst things that can happen to a major leaguer.

Blass was a World Series-winning pitcher with the Pittsburgh Pirates. He threw two complete game victories to help the Bucs win the 1971 Championship including the all-or-nothing Game 7. Knoblauch was a former American League Rookie of the Year second baseman who also won four World Series titles during his career (three with the New York Yankees to go along with his great rookie year in 1991 with the Minnesota Twins).

They both suffered a bizarre and almost unexplainable lack of control while throwing the baseball in their distinguished careers. Many baseball experts believe it was not anything physical but rather a lack of confidence that eventually forced these two to retire prematurely from the game they loved.

TOE-TO-TOE

Boxing is right up there at the top of the most demanding and challenging sports. Putting aside for a moment all of the blood, sweat, and tears that go into training for a fight, boxers must be incredibly tough and equally as confident in the mind. What I'm talking about here is having the mental strength and courage to succeed. Not to mention guts, staying power, grit, determination, and endurance.

There are no time-outs in boxing. The referee isn't going to help you unless stopping the bout will save your health and possibly save your life. Boxers have to combat fatigue and injury as well as their opponent. Show me two boxers of similar size and ability and I'll take the more confident one every time because that boxer expects to win. Just as you should do every day of your life. Anticipate losing and you probably will, but imagine the possibilities when you look ahead to victory.

COACHES AND CONFIDENCE

There is a lot that we can learn from coaches as well in regard to the confidence level of a certain player or team. Think of the football coach who usually chooses to kick the field goal from inside the one-yard line on fourth down. What kind of message does that send to his offensive line? Corporate managers often do the same thing when proverbially "taking the ball out of their players' hands" when a big decision has to be made or an important presentation made to a possible new client.

But ponder the potential outcome of these situations when coaches or managers have faith in their bunch to go for it or let their people decide. What a confidence boost! Powerful stuff right there.

There are many examples of a head coach removing his starting quarterback for poor performance and killing his confidence for the rest of the season. Or, maybe the player just wasn't meant to be an NFL quarterback in the first place.

I love it when I see a quarterback go right back to a receiver the play after he a dropped pass. It's as if the QB is saying, "Hey, man, I believe in you. We'll get it done next time." There's a lesson in there for parents somewhere.

Sports really are a microcosm of society. Consider what losing sports franchises resort to. Logo changes, uniform makeovers, bobblehead giveaways, fireworks nights and, worst of all, a revolving door policy in regard to their players and coaching staff. Just like people who lack confidence, organizations that have a weak process and show no consistency really just lack a belief in what they're trying to accomplish and how they're going to get it done. And it shows in the loss column.

KEY TAKEAWAYS FROM THIS CHAPTER

- Develop a "Why not me?" attitude.

- Ordinary people and organizations can do extraordinary things with a great process.

- Consistently doing the things you believe will get you where you want to go.

- Don't quit—ever.

- Develop a belief that it's working.

- You really can do whatever you decide to do if you believe it.

- Don't lose it once you have it!

- Stay away from gimmicks.

Chapter Nine

INTERVIEW #2: THE ITALIAN-AMERICAN COOK FROM SOUTH PHILLY

Cuz, for me it's all been about passion. When you talk to someone and you ask them what they're doing and they're passionate and successful—it's love. Talk to a guy who's got nothing and he's just putting himself down. But the successful guy is bursting with excitement all the time trying to explain to others what he does for a living.

-Steve "Yo Cuz" Martorano

Steve "Yo Cuz" Martorano started as a club DJ in the 1970s before opening his first sandwich delivery business, which he ran from his apartment in the working-class neighborhood of South Philadelphia. From there he would make the sandwiches, wrap them, take the phone off the hook to personally deliver them, return home, put the phone back on the hook, and wait for the next call. He was a one-man show with an increasingly popular business.

The food became so well liked in South Philly that Martorano decided to open a takeout restaurant in a strip mall. Here he made pizza, sandwiches, pasta dishes, and homemade water ice. A few years later the demand outgrew his location again and Martorano moved to a bigger freestanding sit-down restaurant.

In the early 1990s the economy took a turn for the worse and Steve lost everything. He knew it was time for a change and, in 1993, he moved to Fort Lauderdale, Florida, and opened up a new restaurant. Fast forward to today and Café Martorano has become a worldwide sensation as have his other restaurants in the Rio Casino in Las Vegas and the Hard Rock Casino in Hollywood, Florida.

With tattoos on top of muscles (on top of muscles), this "Italian guy from the neighborhood" looks like no restaurant owner you have ever seen and has taken the craft of cooking to new levels through persistence and hard work. With his self-taught talent, Steve has created a venue in which as owner he is the cook, DJ, and operator. His restaurants offer a unique atmosphere that combines exceptional food with extraordinary music. Guests dine on Italian-American food while watching his favorite movies and listening to classic rock and R&B on a sound system that rivals that of South Beach's hottest clubs.

This rare talent has allowed him to create an ambiance that attracts a clientele ranging from a local, sexy, hip crowd to the sports and entertainment industries' hottest celebrities. Some of Steve's most famous clientele are Tom Cruise, Shaquille O'Neal, Ludacris, and Dan Marino.

Steve shares his tough upbringing as well as some of his favorite recipes in his new book Yo Cuz—My Life, My Food, My Way. Steve has appeared multiple times on the Jimmy Kimmel Live! show as well as Fox and Friends and many others.

Steve's meatballs cost $18 each and if you've had one you probably think they're underpriced. The note to his customers on the bottom of Café Martorano's menu just about says it all. It reads: **ABSOLUTELY NO CHANGES OR SUBSTITUTIONS. Just let me do what I do and don't break balls.**

DS: Steve, can you tell me a little about your childhood?

SM: I'm just an Italian kid who grew up in an Italian-American neighborhood. My father worked for his brothers, driving a truck in their vending business, and went to work every day to earn a paycheck. He couldn't write, he couldn't spell, and he couldn't read. I didn't know that growing up. I didn't even know that we were poor because everybody in the neighborhood kind of lived the same way. You didn't see no fancy cars or anything like that until you left the neighborhood and then there was a whole different world out there.

I went to a Catholic school that was literally paid for by the change my father earned from the vending business. My mother would actually sit around the house counting the change to make sure there was enough to keep me in this school. I didn't do real well in school because I wasn't interested. I actually failed a lot.

Growing up in South Philly we just did what we had to do until we got a little older and realized there was this other world out there. And that other world was me wanting to be a gangster. I would see others in the neighborhood not working as hard as my father did from nine to five every day. These gangsters were living a good life with nice cars and nice clothes; everywhere they went, people opened doors and treated them with respect. That's what I wanted to be. But then I had a couple of uncles go away (to prison) for a while. I have a cousin who is still the longest serving non-violent offender in the history of this country. He's going on twenty-nine years—it's unheard of.

So I looked around and everybody's either going to jail or getting killed. So I had to make a choice. Do I want to drive a truck all day like my father or become a gangster who would end up either getting clipped or going to jail? I decided to cook. Mainly because I like to eat. I started cooking out of my apartment in South Philly. I'd make these flyers and put "Steve's Italian Kitchen" on them. All my friends would laugh at me because they got involved in that other stuff and drove around the neighborhood in fancy cars while I was going around the neighborhood dropping these flyers off in people's mailboxes. Business wasn't real good at first as the phone rarely rang. I had to do something to make money though, so at night I became a DJ in nightclubs.

DS: Do you feel that the way you were raised in South Philly instilled confidence in you to do great things?

SM: The confidence had to come from me. A lot of people are always told good things. But for me it was always bad. It was like "He's never going to amount to nothing," or "He's always failing," and "He ain't gonna be nothing." So if I listened to them I probably would have been a failure. Even today people ask me how it feels to be successful and I tell them, "I don't know—I go to work every day."

DS: On the flip side of the last question, what did you have to overcome in the confidence department to achieve the success you have had?

SM: The more I heard I was never going to amount to anything I would always ask myself, "Well, why not?" It's not no but it's yes and I was like "I'm gonna show you—I'm gonna show you what I can do!" And it was all about believing in me. No matter how many times I was told it would never work, I didn't buy into it.

When I first opened my small restaurant in Florida, it was all pink. I was like "What is this fucking pink?" I'm thinking I'm a guy from Philly—I'm gonna get whacked with all this pink. I wanted it to be black and white. But everybody told me that everything in Florida had to be pink or light blue or that it won't work. But I wanted black and eighteen years later all of my restaurants are black and white.

And I haven't taken any shortcuts with the food. The way I cook is much harder than any other restaurant out there. But I can taste the difference when people take shortcuts and that wasn't for me. People kept telling me, "Steve, your way is too much hard work and takes too much time. People aren't going to wait." Well, guess what. In time, people were waiting two to two and half hours for a table.

People have told me I'm too old to be on TV. I've proved them wrong. I'm doing TV every other month.

So, the confidence comes from people telling me, "No, you can't," and then me saying, "Why not?" and proving them wrong.

DS: Looking back, what were the key elements that made you into the very confident person that you are today?

SM: Cuz, for me it's all been about passion. When you talk to someone and you ask them what they're doing and they're passionate and successful—it's love. Talk to a guy who's got nothing and he's just putting himself down. But the successful guy is bursting with excitement all the time trying to explain to others what he does for a living.

DS: From my research and talking to you I get the sense that you are really driven by the many people who didn't think you could succeed. What role does that play in your life?

SM: Cuz, they're still out there. Stay with me here because I get a little emotional when I talk about this. You see nobody knows.

People don't know how hard it's been from the day I was born until now. I've got to fight every day. Every day I've got to put the gloves on. There's always somebody out there trying to take something away from me. There's always somebody out there writing something negative about me. It gets me mad and it fuels me to prove them wrong.

I've got three restaurants, a line of products that are on the market, and I've got a cooking show that's been funded by one of the biggest companies around. I've done major TV shows and yet people still question me. I'm always afraid that somebody is going to take something away from me and that drives me.

DS: What exactly do you do on a daily basis?

SM: I'm a creature of habit. I only sleep about four hours a night. I don't watch much TV but when I do I watch the Food Network because I figure I can learn something from other great cooks. I wake up in the morning and take my vitamins and then I'll hit the gym for two hours. I do that seven days a week. About 11:00 a.m. I'll do some food shopping while I'm thinking about the things I'm gonna make for Fort Lauderdale. Then I've got to deal with Vegas and the Hard Rock and any issues that came up the night before. Then I answer all my e-mails. Around four o'clock I get to the restaurant and begin prepping up things that I want to make special for that night. I stay there until about seven thirty and then go home and take a quick shower and I'm back there by twenty after eight. I do this seven days a week when I'm in Lauderdale. When I get back, I cook and I try to greet people as they come in. I still care about every dish that goes out of that kitchen. I stay at the restaurant until about twelve thirty and then I go home and answer a few more emails and read some more cookbooks and before you know it it's four o'clock in the morning. Then I go to sleep and that's basically my day.

DS: At what point in your life did you know that you were on to something with this cooking stuff?

SM: When people started waiting for three and a half hours to eat at the Oakland Park (Fort Lauderdale) restaurant. I realized it wasn't just about the food. It's about the movies, it's about the music, it's about people watching. I created something that nobody else was doing. That's when I realized we got something. The TV interviews and stuff like that has just kind of happened. They come to me every other week now wanting me to do a reality show but I'm not interested in all that drama. This isn't Jersey Shore. If you wanna do a show about cooking with an inspirational message then we're fine. But that's not what producers want right now. So I decided to do that myself and the shows are available on my website, cafemartorano.com. I did what I wanted to do, not what they wanted me to do.

DS: What role has confidence played in getting you to where you are today?

SM: It's all that because if you don't have confidence this world will eat you up, spit you out, and keep you down. I've got this saying on my arm that says, "It's not how hard you hit—it's how hard you get hit and keep moving forward." Let me tell you something, cuz, hits are gonna come. Getting knocked down isn't the hard part. Getting up is. People look at that tall mountain and think the hard part is getting to the top. No, the hard part is getting started. People have it all opposite. You gotta fucking believe in yourself!

DS: Can you tell me a little about the effect your level of confidence has on others?

SM: It's the blessing in this whole thing, cuz. I'm just a guy from South Philly with no real education. I've had major actors and ballplayers call and tell me not to pick up the phone because they want to listen to my voice mail message where I thank all the people who told me I couldn't do it. I tell everybody not to listen to those who tell you that you can't. If you've got a passion for what you're doing you can accomplish anything. That's what this country is based on. I get e-mails all the time now from people who have read the book and have told me, "If you could do it then I can do it too!" That's the blessing of being confident. Just the fact that you can make it from nothing to something. People need that today. They need to know that there's hope out there.

DS: What are the sorts of things that have provided you with confidence over the years?

SM: Sinatra used to say that if you can please 50 percent of the people you're ahead of the game. Since I was born, I knew that I was going to be a success. And it's all because of hard work. If I had worked at a car wash I'd have been the best car wash guy you'd ever see. And I recognize that the more successful you become the more humble you've got to be. And it's helped me as I've become more successful to give back. You can't just hoard it, you've got to give back. That's just the law of nature. And it makes you feel good.

DS: What elements tend to knock your confidence level down a notch or two?

SM: It's that little voice that talks to you in your ear sometimes. So you've got to surround yourself with the right people in your life who are going to keep you motivated or else it's a struggle. If you start listening too much to the outside world it can get to you and knock you down and make it hard for you to get back up. You've got to have key people in your life who believe in you.

DS: How has confidence and success in your professional life helped you to become a more confident person in your personal life?

SM: Let me tell you something. I was a no-good motherfucker, cuz. At one point I wanted to be a gangster and then I just wanted to party. In my family, we drank. Somebody got married—we drank. Somebody died—we drank. That's just what it was. I finally grew up about two years ago and haven't had a drink since then. I woke up one day and counted my blessings and said enough's enough. I was sick and tired of being sick and tired.

DS: You've had countless numbers of A-list celebrities rave about your food and the dining experience. How are you so confident that people will love coming to one of your restaurants?

SM: It's my home. When people come to Café Martorano, they're in my house. I let my staff know where to sit them. I don't take requests. Did people pay $500 to see Sinatra and then stand up and yell, "I wanna hear 'Summer Winds'?" No! They paid $500 to hear Frank do what he does. That's what you're paying me for. You're coming here to let me do what I do. And that's all about confidence. And the celebrities respect that because they have to deal with that kind of stuff every day. I told Madonna she couldn't come in. There was already a three-hour wait. I had all these regular people ready to spend their hard-earned money. I told her she had to come back another day. I believe in what I'm doing and I believe that what I'm doing is right. And we're gonna do it my way when you're in my house. When we're in your house we can do it your way.

DS: You're not exactly the typical "sales" guy but no doubt you've had to sell yourself and your concept to get people to come to your restaurants and buy into your "Yo Cuz" brand. Tell me a little bit about how confidence has played a role in that regard.

SM: It's 100 percent. People can feel when you're confident about what you're doing. We have a saying in Philly: "Fake it 'til you make it." When you're dealing with people with real money they want to see a guy who is confident. When we approached the Hard Rock they wanted to make sure that I believed it a million times. And I do. And they in turn believe in me. They know I'm going to be at the top of my game and make sure that the product is consistently right.

DS: What type of things do you do consistently to keep your confidence level as high as possible?

SM: I pray a lot. You have to believe in something. And you gotta do it right. You can't try and hurt somebody. That only works so many times. I'm trying to plant trees that are going to bear good fruit. I'm a man of my word. Cuz, if I shake your hand I don't need a contract. Unfortunately, that doesn't work real well in the world today.

DS: What does the future hold for Steve Martorano?

SM: It's all about the brand, the "Yo Cuz" brand. There's a clothing line, sneakers, urban wear. Plus more food products from Martorano's. Do I want more restaurants? Probably not. I plan on bringing other ventures to my name. And it will always be of the highest quality. There will probably be another book. I've got Jimmy Kimmel saying "Yo Cuz." I own it, it's my brand.

DS: How confident are you that you'll get there?

SM: It's already done. I know it. It's gonna happen. You know how I know? Because I believe. I still have the passion. And I haven't made it yet. That's what keeps driving me. Shaq threw down a million dollars and said let's open up some of these things. I'm not ready for all that yet but I'm coming strong!

DS: Is there anything else you'd like to add that readers of this book would be interested to know?

SM: It's so basic. You've got to believe in yourself and that's the bottom line. The more people that tell you no, the more you say yes. You can be something, but only by believing in yourself. If you don't believe it you'll never get anywhere. I set little goals every day. I don't worry about tomorrow; I worry about today. Let me accomplish my three or four little goals each day and tomorrow will take care of itself.

Chapter Ten

TREAT THE JANITOR LIKE THE CEO AND THE CEO LIKE THE JANITOR (SORT OF)

The man who acquires the ability to take full possession of his own mind may take possession of anything else to which he is justly entitled.

-Andrew Carnegie

Confident people treat everybody with a tremendous amount of respect. They have the ability to quickly and effortlessly strike up friendships with people from all walks of life.

A number of years ago I worked in an office building that was built in the 1960s. Every office and cubicle had its own individual heating and cooling unit. And these things almost never worked. Well, they'd work occasionally, but at the wrong times of the year. The heat would kick on in the summer and the AC would blast you with freezing air in the winter. In order to get your unit fixed you had to call the maintenance office and put in a "work-order." It would literally take weeks and sometimes even months before one of the maintenance guys would ever take a look at it.

Whenever I had a problem with my unit, however, someone would address it within minutes. How so (you might be asking)? Simple; the maintenance guys were my friends and I treated them like the most important people in the world. And people take good care of their friends.

Now let me be perfectly clear about this. I didn't befriend the maintenance guys because I wanted the heating and cooling unit in my office fixed quicker. I befriended them because I liked them and I generally develop quality relationships with all the people I have contact with on a daily basis. That's what confident people do! And besides the differences in our jobs, I had a lot in common with these guys. We all loved sports, bullshitting about politics and current events, as well as checking out the pretty girls! That was before I was married, of course.

YOU'RE JUST AS IMPORTANT AS EVERYONE ELSE—AND SO ARE THEY

The point is that nobody is less or more important than you are and vice versa. Period. I know, some may have more authority and make more money. But that doesn't make them more important. Everybody has a place in this world and when you treat all of them with respect this thing called "karma" usually takes care of you in the long run. Ignore this concept at your own risk.

Kids who were raised the right way by their parents learn this at a very early age. They're nice to everybody regardless of social status, finances, looks, brains, etc. I remind my son, Alex, every morning before going to school to not only "be a leader today" but to "stick up for those who can't or won't stick up for themselves." He's pretty good about doing this even though he's one of the smaller kids in his class.

The sad part is that so few people actually live by this creed. Most kiss the backsides of those "in charge." The corporate world is overflowing with this. It makes me want to chunk every time I see it. It is absolutely nauseating. And the people who do it the most are the ones who don't even recognize that they're doing it.

I've been to regional corporate meetings where all the "wannabes" gather around the head honchos like they're E. F. Hutton spewing some magical advice. GAG! Do they think this helps their career? Trust me—it doesn't! What it does is make you a legitimate "brownnoser." And that's the last thing most great leaders want working for them, someone who is going to agree and hype every idea that the boss has.

If these people could just see themselves on video in these situations it's a good bet they'd be totally embarrassed by their own actions. But maybe not, as these folks aren't the most self-aware individuals on the planet.

DON'T BE SCARED TO DISAGREE WITH THOSE WHO HAVE BIGGER TITLES

I've always taken the opposite path in regard to bosses and people with great authority. Most definitely learn from them if they truly have something of value to teach. But instead of breathlessly hanging on every syllable they're about to utter, I choose instead to treat them like an old pal, one that I may have played ball with back in the day. You know, kid with them and get to know them as a person instead of an icon. Share ideas with them rather than just sit in awe of theirs. Give them a little friendly ribbing from time to time. Let them know that you're intelligent, real, and important—just like they are. No more, no less.

This is all done with respect, mind you. I'm certainly not suggesting that you begin the relationship with a locker room "towel whip" or by telling them "your momma" jokes. However, I am encouraging you to treat them as equals.

It's perfectly OK (and even encouraged) to gracefully disagree with your boss from time to time. This is not something you want to do in front of others and you definitely don't want to get an attitude about it. Just be yourself, speak conversationally, and let him or her know that you have a difference of opinion and here's why. You don't want to push it too far, but the best leaders love to have people on their team who consider and present alternative strategies on occasion.

It's probably not a great idea to be at loggerheads with everything your boss has to say. Be smart about the issues you'd like to challenge. "Choose your battles" doesn't only work with your spouse and kids!

DON'T BE THIS PERSON

Keep in mind that the only way for you to really make a name for yourself is to have original thoughts and ideas. Clones and kiss-asses typically can only get so far up the corporate ladder. These people get lower-level promotions because management sees them as individuals who will carry out their agenda without question. These suck-ups often never get any higher than middle management due to their inability to think independently and actually develop strategies and real-world business solutions on their own. They're fearful of taking risks and making bold moves. All they want to do is preserve their space and not make waves. And these are the people who stick their chests out with an aura of misguided self-importance. This is also called arrogance, which is addressed at length in the next chapter of this book. Don't be this person.

It's interesting to note that when these doormats get put into positions of authority that they just perpetuate themselves over and over again with the same mentality of people they bring on board under them. You see, yes-people don't want too many conflicts or challenges. Which means they certainly don't want someone reporting to them who is going to question their authority from time to time. Blasphemy!

Like so many in the corporate world, I've been both boss and subordinate all at the same time. I've always appreciated when someone disagreed with my stance on an issue in a respectful, thoughtful, and well-presented manner.

On the flip side, I couldn't stomach it when certain people would always utter "I agree" after everything I had to say. How could you possibly see eye to eye with everything I said and did? They didn't. They just don't possess the kahunas to portray what they really feel out of fear that their safe position of relative obscurity may be disrupted. So much for Frank Sinatra's idea of doing it "your way."

STRONG SPINE—SOFT EXTERIOR

Strive to have a spine made of steel all wrapped up in a soft and cuddly exterior made of cotton. Don't compromise your principles. Speak up for yourself and your beliefs. Voice your disagreements on important issues in a respectful yet confident manner, all the while being friendly, approachable, and humble regardless of your position.

Present yourself to the world in this fashion and the welcoming, pleasant, and congenial way that you carry yourself will be reciprocal. People of all social statuses will feel comfortable around you just as you will around them.

I want to be perfectly clear here about this. I'm not just talking about being "friendly" to everyone you come in contact with. That should be a given. You should make an effort to actually develop some sort of relationship with all of the people in your life that you encounter frequently. It doesn't really require a Herculean effort on your part. Just be real, be present, and be a supporting ally for one another. As the saying goes, you have to be a friend before you can have a friend.

UNINTENDED BENEFITS

Hey listen—a great idea is a great idea no matter where it comes from. And very often in the corporate world it will come from those "front line" workers who deal with the everyday realities of the business that the big wigs in their ivory towers have no clue about. And how can you listen to the people in the trenches if you pay them no mind? You can't.

Add to this the fact that these are the people who really know what's going on with everybody in your organization. Who did what to who. Who's looking for another job. Who stole whose accounts or parking space or whatever. Whether you're a manager or not, knowledge is power! Temper this wisdom with the understanding that the best way to play the office politics game is to stay above the fray—always!

As with most things in life, this too perpetuates itself. The stronger your relationships are with those you encounter on a daily basis the more confident you'll be with all people. Meeting new folks will become easier and easier and you'll have gained a greater understanding of what makes people from all walks of life tick. You're not exactly walking in their shoes but at least now you have a much better view of the way they see the world.

Others will begin to view you as someone who can communicate with everybody. And that's just about the best thing anyone could say about you at work. After all, the number one skill employers look for in potential hires is their ability to communicate. Demonstrate this daily by the way you go about your business and your boss and co-workers won't be able to not notice.

And keep in mind, someday you may need your heating and cooling unit checked!

KEY TAKEAWAYS FROM THIS CHAPTER

- People who are genuinely confident with who they are treat everybody with a great amount of respect.

- Nobody is more important than anybody else. Live by this motto and it will serve you well.

- It's OK (and even encouraged) to respectfully disagree with your boss and those with bigger titles than yours.

- Nobody likes a kiss-ass. And you're not doing yourself any favors (like you think) if you are one.

- Develop a spine made of steel with a soft and cuddly exterior made of cotton.

- The front line people are an invaluable resource within your organization. Tap into them.

Chapter Eleven

ARROGANCE DOES NOT EQUAL CONFIDENCE

Nobody can be so amusingly arrogant as a young man who has just discovered an old idea and thinks it is his own.

-Sydney J. Harris

Webster's defines the word arrogant as follows:

- Having or showing an exaggerated opinion of one's own importance, merit, ability, etc...

- Conceited; overbearingly proud

Some people believe there is a fine line between confidence and arrogance. I'm not one of those people. As we examine the differences between the two traits, I believe the case will be made that they really have very little in common.

Displays of arrogance are all around us and unavoidable. Politicians are perfect examples and easy targets for this discussion. Republican, Democrat, Independent. It doesn't matter. They've all been guilty way too often.

Let's review some newsworthy recent examples:

- New Jersey governor Chris Christie (R), who is known for his no-nonsense and cost-cutting ways, recently spent thousands of dollars of taxpayer money to fly by helicopter to catch his son's high school baseball game. On more than one occasion, the governor has publicly stated there needs to be "shared sacrifice" due to the difficult economic climate of our times.

- United States House Rep. Anthony Weiner (D) from New York, who did multiple television interviews one week claiming that his Twitter account was hacked and then the next week admitted that he had sent lewd photos of himself to a young woman thousands of miles away. And he came clean about it only when it became obvious to him he was about to be exposed (sorry for the pun!).

- Mr. Terminator himself and former governor of California Arnold Schwarzenegger (R), who claimed to be a man of family values during his election bid, admitted to impregnating the family's live-in housekeeper at around the same time he was impregnating his wife, Maria Shriver.

And here's a not-so-recent example of political arrogance, but very poignant nonetheless:

- Queen Marie Antoinette was on the throne of France back in the 1700s at a time of much poverty for a majority of her country's citizens. There was a tremendous lack of food. Even bread was hard to come by for many of the poorest French households. Once, after being told that some people in her own country didn't even have bread to eat, the queen reportedly said, "Let them eat cake," ignoring the fact that if they didn't have the money for bread they certainly couldn't afford the more expensive cake.

All of these instances show supreme arrogance. None of these examples has anything to do with confidence. Arrogance is a feeling of superiority over others and is a trait of the ego. Confidence is a feeling of self-worth and is a trait of your belief system.

ARROGANCE AND CONFIDENCE ARE OPPOSITES

Arrogant people tend to want to prove to others that they are better in some way. Smarter, prettier, richer, stronger, etc. . . In reality it usually comes from a deep-down feeling of deficiency in a particular area. A person who exhibits these qualities tries to cover for those weaknesses by putting down others or taking them for fools.

Confident individuals, however, usually have an objective and pragmatic view of who they really are. This has been learned through all of their experiences. Unlike the arrogant crowd, these people aren't threatened when others do well.

Confident people seek out others' opinions. Arrogant folks always know what's best for you. Those who have a high self-worth believe in who they are and their expertise. Those with a bloated opinion of who they are see themselves as worthier and preferred. A confident person loves to compete intensely and respectfully. An arrogant person is often shrewd but cutthroat in these interactions.

A key difference is that truly confident people admit when they've messed up and take steps to correct the issue. Accepting these realities empowers someone to manage shortcomings with poise and decency. Arrogant people tend to compound their imperfections and vices by ignoring them.

CONFIDENCE IS BUILT ON SUBSTANCE—
ARROGANCE IS BUILT ON NONSENSE

As we've discussed at length earlier in this book, confidence is a self-worth belief system built on a foundation of:

- The Mind, Body, and Soul Trifecta

- Surrounding Yourself with Inspirational People

- Developing Courage

- Trusting in the Actions—Results—Beliefs Circle

Arrogance is a manifestation of ignorance. Ignorance of how you're acting and ignorance of how the world sees you.

Think of the most arrogant people you know. I'll bet they are the same folks who don't have a clue as to the opinion that others have about them. Self-important "puffy chest" types who are borderline cartoon characters. These arrogant souls can't seem to get out of their own way.

We all know creatures like this. They are so eager to spew their gibberish (because they want you to believe their opinion is the know all, be all) that they don't realize how foolish they actually appear. These blockheads remind me of the RUN DMC song "You Talk Too Much" from the 1980s. The line from the song that sums them up best is "You talk about people you don't even know and you talk about places you never go. . ."

Ironically, many of these individuals are the same sycophant, wannabe, "yes-men" type of stooges that worship the backsides of their superiors like we talked about in the last chapter. These people could be the impetus for a great Thursday night "must-see TV" sitcom idea!

Here are eight things to avoid doing that arrogant people are famous for:

1. Blame Others
2. "One-up" Everybody
3. Constantly Interrupt
4. Drop Names Off Topic
5. Don't Respect Others' Time
6. Bad-mouth the Competition
7. Demean Everyone
8. Ignore Their Own Weaknesses

CONFIDENCE AND ARROGANCE HAVE VERY DIFFERENT EFFECTS ON OTHERS

Arrogant people have a hard time making great decisions because they view all other opinions as inferior to their own. So not only do they alienate those around them because they have an extremely closed-minded view of the world, but they also bring down the people closest to them emotionally. They don't realize it because they're unable to see how others see them. And, more often than not, others see them as people walking around with a constant cloud over their heads. Arrogance breeds negativity and stifles new ideas, growth, and openness. This is very destructive behavior whether it is in a family setting or on the job.

People with this warped sense of superiority have a propensity to disgust, annoy, and upset those they encounter. Many folks find these blowhards a little too much to stomach. Look around your environment. If you can't figure out who the arrogant one is, it may just be you!

The sports world is strewn with examples of arrogant superstars that were loathed by their teammates. These jerks treated everybody as inferior—management, fans, and the media included.

Names like Barry Bonds, Randy Moss, Ron Artest, and Tiger Woods come immediately to mind. As do Roger Clemens, Ryan Leaf (although far from a superstar), and Ricky Henderson. A discussion of these characters could constitute an entire book of its own.

Some may view arrogant individuals as "overconfident." I look at it a little differently, as I don't believe you can have too much confidence. Your confidence can be misguided, however, and that's what these arrogant SOBs don't understand.

Confident and humble people, on the other hand, tend to raise the mood of a room, as their positive energy and hopeful outlook permeate their environment. These folks have fewer uncertainties about their abilities than most and display it in an approachable, secure, and nonthreatening manner.

Others often see their actions as gutsy or valiant and once in a while even fearless or heroic. Think of a military leader like Norman Schwarzkopf during the Gulf War or a politician such as Rudy Giuliani for the way he handled a post 9/11 New York City. The sports world has given us leaders like Michael Jordan, Mario Lemieux, and Tom Brady (wow does that hurt to type) who have all lifted up their teammates and made everyone around them just a little bit better.

The list of confident leaders is endless. There are people everywhere who aren't household names that make all those they come into daily contact with feel just a little bit better about themselves.

Other people and/or members of a team can't help but gravitate toward trendsetters that ooze a steady stream of self-belief in a respectful and working-class way. These people are attracted like magnets! Confident souls seize the awareness, credence, and admiration of all in the vicinity. Ever wonder how an ugly dude gets a beautiful girl? There's your answer! Of course being independently super rich doesn't hurt either.

Arrogant folks, on the other hand, almost always repel people. Even if their message is a strong one, folks tend to be impervious to those who are overbearing, pompous, and big-headed. The negative aura clouds their content every time. The adverse mood, tone, and vibe are often too much to stand. How you say it is every bit as important (if not more so) than what you're saying. Believe that.

BEWARE OF THE ROLE EGO PLAYS IN THE DIFFERENCES BETWEEN CONFIDENCE AND ARROGANCE

Most successful people have an ego that tells them they're good. And that's not a bad thing. When you are in competitive situations, it's great to feel as if you are better than your opponent. The sport of boxing is an obvious example of this. Many other instances may not be as obvious. Job hunting, dating, courtroom trials, sales contests, kickball, etc. . .

Over-inflation of one's ego lends itself to so many damaging qualities. Selfishness, conceit, and a closed mind are usually at the top of this list. The important thing is to be able to draw a distinction between the problems an over-inflated ego can induce and the benefits that a healthy ego can produce.

Think about the times you've been around people who talk only about themselves and their accomplishments. Not a fun conversation, is it? After just a few minutes, you get the feeling that they're really not interested in you at all. You are just another audience for them to boast to in order to prop up their surprisingly low self-esteem.

Relationship problems often occur with people who have egos that are disproportionate with their real social standing. This is not to suggest that those who have achieved great things are allowed to be pompous jerks as some have become. But the majority of incredibly prosperous and high-achieving people understand the concept that people don't really care how much you know until they know how much you care.

A healthy ego is based on your belief system just as your level of confidence is. This kind of thinking can really catapult someone to awesome accomplishments. It's tempered and based in reality and it's kept in check. These folks want to know how you're doing because they realize it's more difficult to "connect" with strangers plus the fact that they are truly interested in more than just themselves.

An over-inflated ego is based on the misguided premise that it makes perpetrators feel better about themselves by giving off an ambience of eminence and supremacy. These individuals almost never ask how you are because that doesn't fit in with their need to dominate the human interaction dynamic that is taking place.

KEY TAKEAWAYS FROM THIS CHAPTER

- Arrogance and confidence are not even related.

- These are opposite traits. One of them is built on a foundation of substance and the other one is propped up by ignorance and fantasy.

- Confidence attracts others. Arrogance repels them.

- True leaders are confident. Few of the arrogant ones last.

- Ego is not a bad word. Except when it's over-inflated.

Chapter Twelve

INTERVIEW #3: THE PUBLICIST

Confidence is something that lives within you. And if you don't have it then other people can't and won't have confidence in you. Period. At the end of the day you have to decide who you want to be and how people will perceive you in regards to how you feel about yourself.

-Heidi Krupp-Lisiten

Heidi Krupp-Lisiten launched Krupp Kommunications (K2) in 1996 from her studio apartment in Hoboken, New Jersey. Sixteen years later, she is the CEO and founder of a New York City-based award-winning public relations, marketing, and branding agency. Heidi has built K2 into an industry leader with a proven record of creating and executing innovative branding and marketing initiatives that build her clients' businesses.

K2 has placed over sixty-five books on the New York Times bestseller lists, including #1 bestsellers The South Beach Diet and Your Best Life Now. She played an integral role at ABC News 20/20 and amassed an impressive string of production and publicity credits during her tenure at ABC, including her first publicity credit for Barbara Walters. She is a member of Women in Communications, the Public Relations Society of America, American Business Women's Association, Publisher's Publicity Association, and the National Association of Female Executives, and she serves as a board member for the Books for a Better Life Awards and Goddard. Heidi resides in New York with her husband, Darren, and newborn son, Caden.

DS: Heidi, can you tell me a little about your childhood?

HKL: I was adopted. My father drives a taxicab and my mother has always worked in a clothing store. They've been together for like sixty years. My dad wasn't really home a lot, but he would make it a point to spend Saturdays with me. My childhood definitely helped shape my future. My dad makes friends with everyone who enters his cab. He usually ends up knowing their whole life story by the time they pay their fare. My mother is and was the proverbial "mouth of the south." She was a publicist without knowing it. It's easy to see where I came from, huh? I went to a private grade school, which I know now we probably couldn't afford. But my parents wanted only the best for me so they sacrificed.

DS: What have you had to overcome in the confidence department in order to achieve the success you have had?

HKL: I don't think you ever really overcome. Even some of the great thought leaders I work with have bad days. But just remembering where I came from helps to ground me and gives me strength. Being focused on where I wanted to go kept my confidence in line.

DS: What was some of the best advice you've ever received?

HKL: One of my mentors, Jan Miller, used to tell me to "act the part" and to go to places that are influential so that I may become influential too. I started my quest to "own the world" with breakfast at the St. Regis. I was shocked that a breakfast for one person could end up being like fifty dollars. I'm thinking to myself, "Is she going to pay for this breakfast?" But she was absolutely right. I had to act and believe that I belonged there. Her point was that you are entitled and allowed to live the life that you want and deserve. One time, while I was working for 20/20, Barbara Walters told me you have to look yourself in the mirror and believe in what you're selling. I've taken that to heart. If I don't believe it how can I expect anyone else to, right?

DS: What are some of the key elements that have made you into a very confident person and allowed you to accomplish such a high level of success?

HKL: Love is at the top of the list and that came from my parents. They were (and are) my cheerleaders who have always given me massive support. Everybody needs a few great mentors and I've been fortunate to have two of the best in Tony Robbins and Jan Miller. I've got the greatest friends in the world. And my best friend, my husband, Darren, is my rock who is tenacious with his positivity. Especially on those days when I need a little extra push.

DS: How did you start Krupp Kommunications and what role did confidence play in that?

HKL: During my time at 20/20 I was invited to Catherine Crier's wedding. Jan Miller was Catherine's literary agent and told me how she represented well-known people like Stephen Covey and Anthony Robbins. Then Jan asked me to come and work for her. I passed on that opportunity but I never forgot Jan telling me that I should open up my own PR firm and that it would take about five thousand dollars to make that happen. A few months later, out of the blue, a woman offered me exactly five thousand dollars for my 1989 Toyota Celica which my grandmother had left for me. So I jumped at the deal and the rest, as they say, is history.

DS: What exactly do you do on a daily basis?

HKL: Every single day is vastly different than the day before in my universe. But the one thing I do consistently all the time is read like crazy, newspapers and magazines mostly. I need to know what's going on in the world!

DS: At what point did you realize that you were on to something with this PR stuff?

HKL: Reba McEntire was interviewed for the show my very first week working for 20/20. I went outside of our normal process and got some great PR and results for us. Management wasn't real happy that I made up my own rules but they were thrilled with the outcome. I knew right then and there that this was for me. I was like "This is easy and fun!" I didn't realize until that moment what a publicist really was. That was the point in time I knew this was my destiny. Of course, I had no idea then that someday I'd actually own an award-winning agency. I now understand that I've actually been doing this kind of stuff my whole life.

DS: What role did confidence play in that realization?

HKL: Confidence has played a huge role in all of this. The more results I got the better I kept feeling about what I was doing. It perpetuates itself.

DS: Can you tell me a little about the effect your level of confidence has on others?

HKL: It has a massive effect. People can tell immediately that I believe in me, so they also believe in me. And then the word spreads. We've never done any advertising or marketing. Its been all referrals and word of mouth.

DS: What sorts of things have provided you with a confidence boost throughout the years?

HKL: Your track record gives you confidence and I'm living proof of that. Once you've had a taste of it you want to keep going. Of course when you receive compliments and great praise, that helps too. But in this business nothing shoots your confidence through the roof more than having a book you've worked with become a #1 best seller!

DS: What elements tend to knock your confidence level down a notch or two from time to time?

HKL: Second-guessing yourself. Self-doubt. Getting stuck in reflection mode sometimes knocks me down a little. But I've learned from Tony Robbins that what you focus on is what you become. He gave me the best line ever. He said, "Heidi, problems are gifts." So whenever there's a problem I decide not to wallow in it but celebrate it. I don't exactly throw a party for my problems but I do think that that's when I'm at my best. There's an opportunity in there somewhere. Chaos allows me to clear it and then put things back in order and start over.

DS: Has confidence in your professional life helped you to become a more confident person in your personal life?

HKL: Like all of us I'm a work in progress. But it absolutely has transferred over. And I'm a mother now. And I know that just like in business I'll learn what I need to know to succeed in that role too.

DS: You've helped over sixty authors ascend to #1 on the New York Times bestsellers list. How are you so confident that media outlets will buy into your thought process?

HKL: I've developed great relationships with the media and I feel very comfortable as well as confident that when I tell them I've got something great they believe me. And they believe me only because I believe in my heart that it's going to be valuable for their audience.

DS: What do you do on a consistent basis to keep your confidence level as high as possible?

HKL: I repeat mantras! And my favorite one is "All I need is within me now!" And then I work out.

DS: What does the future hold for Heidi Krupp-Lisiten?

HKL: I'm going to continue to build global brands that make a difference in the world. And who knows, maybe we'll do a reality show of my life. Wouldn't that be something?

DS: Anything else you'd like to add that readers of this book would be interested to know?

HKL: Absolutely. Confidence is something that lives within you. And if you don't have it then other people can't and won't have confidence in you. Period. At the end of the day you have to decide who you want to be and how people will perceive you in regards to how you feel about yourself.

Chapter Thirteen

SAY THIS TO GET THAT JOB AND THEN EXCEL AT IT!

Inaction breeds doubt and fear. Action breeds confidence and courage. If you want to conquer fear, do not sit home and think about it. Go out and get busy.

-Dale Carnegie

This is a book about confidence but it's not always only about your confidence that's important in helping you reach your goals. No, many times in life it's the confidence that others have in you that is just as vital as the confidence you have in yourself. Never is this more imperative than when you are interviewing for and then starting a new job. Sure, you need to feel great about yourself and believe that you're the best option for them. But in these situations it's just as essential that they feel the same way about you!

In this chapter, I am going to give you specific words to say in a job interview that will immediately separate yourself from 99.9 percent of all of the other candidates. And once hired, you better still have that high degree of confidence that you can succeed.

Think about it; you don't want to just survive there, you want to thrive. We'll take a closer look at some strategies while also going over four of the top questions to constantly ask yourself in order to stay motivated on the job. And then, you are going to fire yourself!

INTERVIEW ANSWERS THAT SET YOU APART

As someone who has led sales departments for quite a long time and has interviewed thousands of potential candidates throughout the years, believe me when I tell you I've heard it all. Some of the responses were very surprising. Replies like "Is it OK if I smoke?" and "Give me a minute while I take this call," and "I really don't like working that closely with other people," and "It took me forever to get here." Those kinds of answers range from the ridiculous to the sublime.

Almost as bad are the responses that are totally self-serving to the job seekers themselves. This includes bragging, boasting, and complaining. A job interview is the time to highlight your career accomplishments and instill confidence in the prospective employer. In these situations, it's very important not to come across as cocky or arrogant. They key here is to make your future employer feel great in the belief that the company will achieve awesome things by having you on board. The best way to do this is twofold:

1) Communicate to the interviewer that you are able to quickly identify and understand what the key success metrics are. Things such as:

   - What are the top five criteria I'll be evaluated on and what tangible results is the company looking for in those areas?

- Is there a process in place to achieve that result or am I to develop a new and better one?

- What works and what doesn't work in this position?

- What are the time frames for achieving these results?

A great example of a perfect answer to the question "Why should we hire you?" to a potential salesperson would be "I understand my ratios. In my current position, I'm asked to produce X amount of sales each month so I work backward from there. Over time I've figured out that it takes me X number of cold calls to get an appointment and I eventually close X number out of the prospects that I've met with. My average sale is $X, which means I need X number of sales to reach my monthly quota. And I know that as long as I stick to the formula I'll either make my goals or be pretty darn close every month."

2) Inform the interviewer that you are so confident in your abilities that you're willing to prove it to them risk-free. You heard me right—you're willing to work for free. Say something like this: "This is truly a great opportunity and I feel strongly that I can help the company not just meet but exceed their objectives. Let's do this. Bring me on board for fifteen, thirty, or forty-five days—whatever you're comfortable with—and don't pay me a thing. At the end of that time, and only if you're comfortable with what you've seen so far, we'll discuss a compensation package that we're both comfortable with. Fair enough?"

Wow, now that's powerful stuff right there! And they'll probably be so impressed with you at this point that they'll pay you from day one.

Hardly anybody else will ever do this. You have to have Rare Confidence to pull that off. But think about it. You'll immediately set yourself up as unique and put distance between you and the other candidates. Instead of putting all the risk on the company, you'll let them know in no uncertain terms that you're willing to take the gamble because you're that sure that they are going to like what they see.

It takes a lot of chutzpah to do this and most won't but most are average. And again, there's a lot of competition in this world if you're average, but not so much for those on top.

The easiest and most genuine way to be credible and achieve your dreams is by losing the self-serving nonsense and instead transferring the benefit to those you are communicating with.

NOW IT'S TIME TO SHINE

Congrats! You got the job! Now what? I'll tell you what. Now you've got to over-deliver on the promises you made about yourself. You certainly don't want to be remembered as a blowhard who only talks a good game, do you? The best possible way to succeed on the job is this: rely on your work ethic, not your talent.

Back in the 1990s, I worked for a company called CEI (Computer Enterprises, Inc.). We brought contract programmers over from India to work in American companies at a time when the United States had a severe lack of this type of talent.

Our job as a sales executive was to make tons and tons of outgoing phone calls to identify opportunities within American companies for these types of positions. We had a company standard of one hundred (documented) outgoing phone calls a day. Every salesperson there struggled with that number as well as their sales quota. And that meant smaller commission checks. The day that I showed up there, I looked around and I said to myself, "They're all good people, but they have nothing on me. I'm gonna outwork them all."

You see, you can't suppress your talent (and why in the world would you want to?). You just don't want to rely on it. So I went ahead and averaged over two hundred outgoing phone calls a day. I got in the office at about 6:30 a.m. and would have one hundred calls in by 11:00 a.m. when I went to lunch. I was able to leave every day by about four in the afternoon because I had made over two hundred calls, but more importantly, I was making my quota as well as big, fat commission checks.

Don't rely on your talent, rely on your work ethic. It will show right through. And the harder you work, the more opportunities you're giving your talent to do its thing. Try this the first day at your new job. Look around, check everything and everybody out, and then intentionally ask yourself what anybody else there has on you. Are they better looking, bigger, faster, stronger? Does that even matter in your line of work? Other than the experience, which you'll get soon enough, I'll wager the typical answer is "None of these people have anything on me!"

Remember the success formula I talked about earlier in the book:

COMPETENCE + FREQUENCY = SUCCESS

It really is that simple, yet so many people complicate their lives and their jobs by looking for a magic pill that doesn't exist. The less you believe in your abilities the more you find yourself searching for that drug. Remember, rely on your work ethic, which equates to how frequently you perform those actions that are part of your job's recognized success matrix. Add to the mix the MIND element of the MIND, BODY, and SOUL foundation to a more confident you and you're well on your way to doing a great job at work.

THINK IN TERMS OF "US" AND "WE" INSTEAD OF "THEY" AND "THEM"

Confident employees align themselves with the company that employs them as well as that organization's mission and objectives. People who complain all the time and are self-serving isolate themselves from what the company is really all about. Think of the electric company women I talked about earlier that I would always run into on my smoke breaks.

Years ago, I worked for IRIS Technologies as the director of sports sales for their Landro Play Analyzer division. Our CEO was a guy by the name of Jerry Salandro. What a sharp dude he was. I learned a ton from him.

One year Jerry won the Western Pennsylvania Ethical Businessperson of the Year award and gave an incredible speech on morals in the workplace. One part about his amazing speech that I'll always remember is his position that management and employees alike have to understand that they are the company. Jerry used to mention that when he heard someone in the company refer to the organization as "they" or "them," something was wrong. I couldn't agree with him more. Trust me when I tell you that management would always rather have employees that refer to the company as "we" and "us." It takes confidence and trust in each part of the management/employee equation to get to that point. Jerry called it "synergy". I call it a well-oiled machine.

MAKE MISTAKES, JUST MAKE 'EM FAST

"Paralysis by analysis" is a term that's often used when someone is frozen into a state of inaction because they're over-thinking something. It happens millions and millions of times each day in office buildings around the world. Coming from a sales background, I will tell you this is the easiest way to low commission checks and an entranceway to your manager's doghouse.

Sales isn't rocket science and I'll bet your industry isn't either. Remember Michael Jordan saying, "I've failed over and over and over again in my life and that's why I succeed." And Wayne Gretzky so famously uttered that "you miss 100 percent of the shots you don't take." The point is it's hard to mess things up terribly when you're trying to create new opportunities and working at a sprinter's pace.

What's the worst thing that can happen? They'll say no, which will get you closer to the eventual yes. Am I right? And this doesn't just work in sales. As a matter of fact, it works in most fields. But not all of them, of course. For example, my wife, Lisa, is a CPA. If she works too fast, a mistake can cost her client a lot of money. And I know you don't want your surgeon working fast and making mistakes in the middle of an operation. But you get the drift.

I've seen people lose their jobs because of fear—fear to act, fear of what to say, fear of rejection, fear of how to handle an anticipated situation that may never even arise. Confident people work through their fears and learn how to overcome them. People who don't believe in themselves have a really hard time with this.

TAKE THE RESPONSIBILITY AND THE BLAME

A surefire way to show your boss that you're a "go-to" person in the office is to step up in the responsibility department. Take culpability when something goes wrong and vow that you'll see to it that it doesn't happen again. Come forward when there's a tough problem to solve and volunteer to develop a process so that it either doesn't happen again or that you have a success system in place if it does.

You know the theory. Need something done? Then give it to the busiest person you know and he or she will figure out a way to get it done. These folks are the opposite of the employees that seem to have a constant case of "it's not my job-itis." We all know too many of these people. They're the ones who look for any excuse to get out of doing work. Not a good trait to have, especially for those who aspire to greater things. Take responsibility, and then make it happen. And then you'll just have to deal with all the good things that will surely follow.

Along these same lines, you need to be really careful about placing blame. Over time, your work ethic and your performance will speak for themselves. By coming forward and accepting blame for something that you may have played only a small role in will help to position you as a leader. That's part of what confident people do. Those with average or below-average self-esteem don't believe they can overcome their mistakes. Instead, they deflect or shift blame. They don't realize that it's just a smoke screen that most people can easily see through.

STAY ABOVE THE FRAY

Malcontents, cliques, and office politics. They all can act like a terrible disease that spreads easily throughout an office and a company. If you've got more than just a few people at your workplace then there's little doubt that you have these phenomena as well. It goes without saying, but I'm gonna say it anyway, that when starting a new job avoid all of the above like the plague. Only bad things happen when you get involved in these things, especially too soon.

Life's natural progression will have you gravitate to some of the people you work with and you'll keep your distance from others in due time. Everybody needs to have friendly relationships in the workplace and it helps to get you through long days and to keep your sanity. But the most important thing to remember is that this is work and job performance has to come first. There will come a time when you will be able to decide whom to strategically align yourself with. They should be like-minded people who management also sees favorably.

The malcontents and the complainers may try to recruit you early on because misery loves company. It's perfectly OK and even encouraged to have great working relationships with them too. Just be careful not to get too close to them, as bad things will eventually happen.

First off, and most critical to recognize, is to revisit who's in your Posse of Inspiration. Is this person worthy? Keep in mind that over time you'll have many of the same attributes as those that are in your posse. Secondly, do you really want the people who are making the decisions at your company to put you in the same category in their minds as this other chronic complainer? I didn't think so.

Remember that the employer/employee relationship should always be mutually beneficial. Long gone are the days when corporations keep people around that aren't pulling their weight. Feelings and sentiment go only so far and it goes both ways. Obviously, an employee can outgrow this relationship also. Confident people have a better sense of when it's time to make a move and they truly believe that the next chapter in their life will be even bigger and better. Individuals with low self-esteem will stay in a bad job the way they would stay in a bad relationship. Familiarity breeds contempt and these folks are usually just too scared to make a move.

STAYING MOTIVATED FOR THE LONG HAUL

As you've probably noticed by now, many of the concepts in this book overlap from chapter to chapter and I'm about to do it again. Let's say you have a great job that you've been at for a number of years. You've got strong relationships with clients and co-workers and your boss thinks highly of you. Yet there are days where the repetition and same old nonsense gets you down. I've been there and I know the feeling well. Well, this is where the SOUL part of the MIND, BODY, and SOUL Confidence Foundation Pyramid to your self-esteem belief system comes into play again.

Motivation comes from within. Although others can inspire you, it's up to you to stay focused and upbeat in order to put your best effort forward from day to day.

HERE ARE THE FOUR QUESTIONS TO ASK YOURSELF TO STAY MOTIVATED ON THE JOB:

- Am I doing all I can to provide the best life possible for my family?

- If my kids could see me at work, would they be proud of me?

- Are my actions of today going to advance my career position in the days ahead?

- Am I respected because of what I repeatedly do?

Be honest with yourself, as the answers to these questions will provide you with that extra something that you'll need to keep on keeping on.

FIRE YOURSELF!

Imagine if you got fired on the last day of every month. Then your boss tells you on the first day of the next month you will have the opportunity to reapply for your position. But keep in mind that your application is going to be based on the totality of your performance over the last thirty days. This includes your results, your attitude, your work ethic, etc. And to make it tougher on you, you'll be up against some extremely strong candidates.

Although you probably wouldn't enjoy working under that sort of pressure from the outside, it's an awesome strategy for you to use internally inside of your head. Fire yourself every month! Think about it, in today's economy it's not a bad idea to make yourself "fireproof" and this technique is a great place to start.

KEY TAKEAWAYS FROM THIS CHAPTER

- Your employer's confidence in you is just as important at work as your confidence in yourself.

- Communicate in a job interview that you value your employer's success metrics.

- Shift the risk to you in order to make it easier for the employer to say, "You're hired!"

- Rely on your work ethic, not your talent.

- It's OK to make mistakes; just make them fast!

- Fire yourself every month.

Chapter Fourteen

THE ESSENCE OF COOL

Nothing gives one person so much advantage over another as to remain always cool and unruffled under all circumstances.

-Thomas Jefferson

UrbanDictionary.com defines cool this way:

"Socially appealing; used to describe any behavior, object, ability, or quality contributing to one's social prowess."

Not so fast with that, I say.

Confidence breeds cool the same way exercise produces muscles. The way hard work yields success. The way scoring more points than the other team manufactures wins.

One definitely comes before the other. Show me someone trying to be cool who lacks self-esteem and I'll show you a phony. An impostor. A pretender, an imitator, a trickster. A swindler, a fake, a sham. A phony, a scammer, an actor. A wannabe who's just perpetrating a fraud.

Sure, even those who lack confidence can "play it cool" in stressful situations. Some can still "be cool" when conflict arises. Many can even "keep their cool" when all others around them are losing theirs. But do they have the "essence"? Are they truly "cool"?

There is no single definition of what it means to be cool. Some see it as an aesthetic attraction. To fascinate the fancy of others. To tempt and entice with a pleasing visual look. Think pop culture kind of stuff. If you have kids, the annual rite of back-to-school shopping comes immediately to mind. But how cool is it really to wear the same gear as the other popular kids? And use the same words? And have your boxer shorts stick out of your jeans? OK, let's not go there.

Another school of thought contends that being cool is nothing more than a behavioral attribute. Kind of like the way subcultures communicate with one another. They have their own "language" that only they can really understand. From the way they talk to the way they move and even the declaration of expressions they show on their face.

This type of cool is born from the habits of people who usually have a problem with some type of authority and it manifests itself in unique verbal and nonverbal ways of conveyance among the peer group. Often, these transmissions occur in a way that the establishment doesn't understand. This way the group's members can question those in power without the fear of retribution. Think Hell's Angels, Crips and Bloods, and prisoners working on a chain gang. Now also think regular everyday employees communicating with each other in a way management doesn't recognize or interpret. And of course there's the teenager versus parent relationship that very often has a similar dynamic.

Still, others think the fundamental quality of cool is really just one's conditions and circumstances of existence; being at peace with yourself while at the same time avoiding antagonism and friction.

Many folks misinterpret the idea of being cool with the concept of being popular. There's no question that at times they do go hand in hand. Think back to high school when there were the cool kids. You know, the popular kids. But wait a minute. Weren't some of those kids jerks, bullies, and bitches? That ain't cool. Not to mention the fact that in that group were probably some materialistic two-faced clones, huh? So let's call it what it is. Popular doesn't always equal cool.

BEING AUTHENTIC IS WHAT IT'S ALL ABOUT

I believe that the only way to truly be cool is to be the most authentic "you" possible. People don't really like or admire someone who is a second-rate version of someone else. Unfortunately, you see personality copycats everywhere. They're all over the American workforce. Schools have always been a breeding ground for this type of "if I don't have a great personality let me try to mimic yours" mentality. But everyone loves and is attracted to those who are real to the core.

The coolest people I know are also the most confident. These are regular humans just like you and me. What sets them apart is that they are so comfortable in their own skin that others feed off it. There's nothing like an original.

These men, women, and children (yes, kids can be cool at a very early age) rarely concern themselves with how they're viewed by the "crowd". They're the ones who recognize that what others think of them is really none of their business.

Mix in some kindness, a little empathy, a strong backbone, and stellar character and you've got one pretty cool dude or dudette right there!

Cool is distinctiveness and singularity to go along with that high dose of self-esteem. The coolest people are also the truly unique people. It's impossible to be cool when you're too busy trying to be like others.

Back in the day, I worked with a guy who epitomized this. He was a great person and a hard worker. A good family man with strong values. He always arrived early and never shied away from a tough project. The only problem was that he often tried to be somebody he wasn't and it showed. He was the best at who he was but failed miserably at trying to be like others.

I'd be walking in the hallway and hear him repeat my words verbatim to someone else. And you could tell that he was struggling to get it out because it wasn't really him talking. He would actually even try to dress like me at times. I'd have to out-think him getting dressed in the morning knowing that, if I didn't, we might end up looking like the Doublemint Twins. Not a good look—trust me.

Be yourself and be the best at it. That's all that others want out of you. Humans are wired to detect a phony instantly. You get talked about if you're a counterfeit version of somebody else. Not to mention that people won't take you seriously. And the bottom line is it's a huge turnoff.

HAVE A COOL STRATEGY—BE S.M.O.O.T.H.

The coolest people I've ever known look like they've never put two seconds into thinking about how they got that way. And there's a good chance they didn't. There are specific things you can do, however, to be as cool as the proverbial cucumber. And remember that these all work in concert with one another. Leave any of them out at your own risk.

S: **Show** Your Curiosity In Others

- This isn't about you. It has to be all about them—at least initially. Not only do you have to show them that you care, but it sure helps if you genuinely do.

- You never have a second chance to make a first impression. Look them in the eye, say their name, and let them know with all sincerity what an absolute pleasure it is to be meeting them at this moment.

- Be inquisitive. Who are they? Do they have kids? What do they do for a living? What do they love to do for fun? What's their passion?

- Be present by really listening. Not by pretending to listen. Focus only on the other person in the one-on-one dynamic.

- Show them courtesy and admiration even if you disagree with their point of view. It's called respect.

- Extend sincere praise. Give them some props, man! And do it in a way that indicates you're not fishing for the same in return.

M: **Mandate** That You're Always Putting The Best You Forward

- Look the part! Present yourself in a confident manner. You don't necessarily always have to dress to impress but you should dress to feel great. But make sure you're comfortable in your clothes. And I'm not just talking about the proper fit. This will reveal itself into presenting a more confident you. And that's half the battle.

- Take care of your body as we talked about back in the MIND, BODY, and SOUL chapter. It's where you live.

- Be humble for goodness sakes! Pretension and ostentatiousness suck.

- Be friendly, welcoming, agreeable, congenial, and pleasant. In other words, be approachable.

O: **Optimism** Reigns Supreme

- You've got to believe that today's the day you'll win the Powerball Lottery—even if you don't play!

- Nothing is more magnetic in terms of personality traits than being around someone who truly believes that tomorrow is gonna be great—and the next day will be even better!

- Never complain out loud. It's not becoming. And it's certainly not cool.

- "If you think you can or think you can't—you're still right!" How true.

- Consider how politicians get elected. They do it primarily by promising hope for a better tomorrow. And people flock to them. Too bad so many of them are lying hypocrites.

O: **Originality** Is The Name Of The Game

- Wear the comfort of being imperfect all over your face and body.

- Accept yourself as a flawed and incomplete character. Nobody's perfect!

- Be "special" at being you.

- Stop trying to "prove" yourselves to others.

- Remember that communicating with others is a contact sport!

- The minute you try to act like someone else is the exact moment when you will have "jumped the shark" with the person you're communicating with.

T: **Teeth**—Smile And Show Some

- It's been said that the easiest and fastest way known to humankind to become better looking instantly is to smile!

- It's got to be genuine and not smarmy or condescending as if to say, "Look how much better than you I am," or "Look at how much money I have."

- When you smile the whole world smiles back at you. Smiles are contagious. I taught my son, Alex, this when he was in kindergarten. He came home from school one day and said, "Daddy, you were right. I smiled at Mrs. Wedner and she smiled right back at me." How cool is that!

- Smiles let people know they are valued, recognized, and accepted.

- A well-placed smile can encourage and calm. Pass it on, it's free, you know.

H: **Have** An Opinion

- Confident and cool people aren't wallflowers. They have opinions on things. They take stances. But they do it in respectful ways.

- Stay abreast of world events. Know what's going on in your community and your industry. Be able to intelligently talk about almost anything.

- Don't act as if you know what you're talking about when you don't. You're credibility will be gone in an instant and forever with that person.

- Nobody respects a one-trick pony. Cultivate diversified points of view and interests like Bond. James Bond.

- Cool people with an abundance of confidence aren't easily swayed by peer pressure. Be true to you, your values, and your beliefs. Take a cue again from the politicians. Flip-flopping doesn't work really well for them either.

KEY TAKEAWAYS FROM THIS CHAPTER

- Cool comes after confidence the way muscles come after exercise.

- There are many different schools of thought as to what it really means to be cool.

- Authenticity and comfort in your own skin are a significant foundation for coolness.

- Never be a second-rate version of someone else.

- Be S.M.O.O.T.H.

Chapter Fifteen

INTERVIEW #4: THE GUINNESS WORLD RECORD HOLDER

I sought out other world record holders. I hunted them down, literally. I modeled their strategies and also synthesized my own to fill in the gaps from what they were not telling me. I became "self-aware" of my memory and deliberately sought to improve it. I read tens of thousands of articles on academic psychology and sought out puzzled professors around the world to tell them how I was doing, what I was doing, and how I was fast becoming amazing with my memory. Therefore, in summary, I used a fusion approach and this all culminated in the coveted title of "Guinness World Record Holder For Memory."

-Adel Anwar

Adel Anwar is a lawyer (and black belt) who is listed in the Guinness Book of World Records for his feats of memory. He is a world expert on the practical use of the "brain computer" for personal, professional, and organizational results. Adel speaks regularly to audiences around the globe on the capabilities of human brainpower as well as on leadership strategies. His numerous clients in the petroleum industry have successfully implemented a number of his unique tactics.

Among other disciplines that Adel has garnered expert status on are business, wealth and investment, book-blasting speed-reading, philosophy, human neuropsychology, and Tae Kwon Do. It's no wonder that one of his favorite quotes is Einstein's "Great ideas often receive violent opposition from mediocre minds."

DS: Adel, can you tell me a little about your childhood?

AA: I left home very young and ended up growing up in British private boarding schools. My parents wanted me to be the quintessential officer and a gentleman, particularly a doctor. I was the opposite at age six!

DS: Do you feel that the way you were raised instilled confidence in you to do great things?

AA: Yes. My parents had great visions for me, specifically to be a doctor like my dad. They told me good things, but like any parents, their motivational strategy was not always right. It was sometimes darn wrong, and caused a sense of rebellion within me as I got older.

DS: On the flip side of the last question, what did you have to overcome in the confidence department to achieve the success you have had?

AA: I had to immerse myself in areas of my life where I was not doing well. Therefore, in sports, I became a Tae Kwon Do champ. In meeting ladies, I became a stud! This is after years of the opposite. In academia, I became very proficient at learning, treating it like sports—a complete turnaround from an "F" type of life!

DS: Looking back, what were the key elements that made you into a very confident person that allowed you to accomplish record-breaking feats?

AA: Above I said "going for it, persisting and immersion." But all this went through the ceiling and blasted off due to learning and seminars about practical human psychology. So there are two ways to get confident and competent:

Method 1: To gain competence with practice resulting in confidence.

Method 2: To start out with confidence, and therefore persist at something to gain competence.

In reality, in "systems thinking," both interact with each other and feed back off of each other in a "feedback loop." This is easy to see in a diagram, a little harder in mere words here.

DS: How did you become the Guinness World Record Holder for human memory?

AA: I sought out other world record holders. I hunted them down, literally. I modeled their strategies and also synthesized my own to fill in the gaps from what they were not telling me. I became "self-aware" of my memory and deliberately sought to improve it. I read tens of thousands of articles on academic psychology and sought out puzzled professors around the world to tell them how I was doing, what I was doing, and how I was fast becoming amazing with my memory. Therefore, in summary, I used a fusion approach and this all culminated in the coveted title of "Guinness World Record Holder For Memory."

DS: What exactly is the record that you hold (or held)?

AA: There are various world record titles for memory. I could do any one of them to a very high standard such as memorize a deck of cards in less than a minute flat! However, I chose to have "random objects" put to me to beat the previous record. I recalled 500 percent more random objects than an average person under those rigorous test conditions. Objects were called out one by one, I was blindfolded, and they were called out one-half second at a time. I had to recall them consecutively in the order they were given to me, 100 percent correct (one mistake and it is zero score), and immediately! It was daunting in front of a live studio audience. But I did it!

DS: At what point in your life did you realize that you were on to something with this memory stuff?

AA: The reason I started with memory is because I had gotten myself into law school! I was so proud of myself. However, I knew that I would not survive the stress of a legal education without being brilliant with the use of my mind. So that was the starting point and motivation to master my memory!

DS: What role did confidence play in that?

AA: I totally believed that there were techniques out there and I had a flexible mind-set to learn more. Research shows that many intelligent people fall into a fixed mind-set, thinking you've either got it or not (like IQ). This has been proven by academic scientists to be nonsense and a myth of a bygone industrial age era! Today, we know the brain is malleable and with training one can achieve mastery in almost any area.

Curiously, even many growth-oriented people wish to hold onto the myth of "exclusivity" genes when it comes to the arts: music, singing, painting, or the myth of genius. Geniuses are always those that have rigorously practiced their art—with no exceptions found to date "whatsoever"! I too practiced the science of memory. The good news is that with memory it is ridiculously simple. Minimal practice is required to develop a photographic memory.

DS: Can you tell me a little about the system of memory that you teach?

AA: I cannot, as it is a trade secret! I can say it involves using a fusion approach based upon every single result and test found in universities' psychology departments. Everything is known, but I have packaged it in a usable, practical way!

DS: Can anyone learn this?

AA: Yes. The youngest person I taught was seven years old. She was screaming out medical terms by the end of one day and it really shocked her parents. The oldest was an aged lady with an oxygen tank. She had dementia but she also shocked her family by being able to remember and recall whatever she put her mind to. And that too was based on just one intense day!

DS: What are the sorts of things that have provided you with confidence over the years?

AA: Sports. Professional speaking. Personal health and fitness. Great Saturday Night Fever moments! Talking to strangers. And sales results!

DS: What elements tend to knock your confidence level down a notch or two?

AA: I think rejection knocks everyone down a little. Any time one's expectations are thwarted. The brain is set up as an expectation mechanism as that is highly advantageous to survival (think about it)! However we must "be aware" and "remind ourselves" that being rejected is perfectly normal, and it is never the wrong "F" word—failure, but the right "F" word—feedback. So one must say "next" and try and try again!

DS: How have confidence and success in your professional life helped you to become a more confident person in your personal life?

AA: I have carved out a unique and international entrepreneurial career, living life on my own terms. That has been great! I have been able to live in great U.S. locations from Southern California to New York. I have moved to places with no friends and alone but created friends and a home. I've had to do this several times in my life. Pure adventure!

DS: You've taught your system around the world. How are you so confident that audiences will buy into your thought process?

AA: I do demonstrations that blow their minds by being able to remember anything they throw at me from their own unique expert knowledge and professional fields. They don't understand how I can operate like a machine! But then it gets interesting when I share a technique or two and instantly they witness their own photographic memory. This is enough to push them over the edge and they want to know more. But I also demonstrate how my clients have made literally millions of dollars due to using the mind in a better way. When I say "millions," please be aware, this is no figure of speech. I mean "millions," documented and proven by Fortune 500 companies which they can check for themselves!

DS: You're not exactly the typical "sales" guy, but I imagine that you've had to sell yourself and your services to some degree to get hired by clients. Tell me a little bit about how confidence has played a role in that regard.

AA: Every leader must be a seller of an idea, a concept, or a product. One explores through natural questions in conversation. If there is no fit, then one moves on. If there is a fit then one makes an offer to form a business relationship. This is quite different to beating people over the head as in the past. Confidence, therefore, means having inner self-esteem: being happy, proud, persistent, and willing to help people. To offer value, to believe in one's product, but not to badger them or somehow force them. Instead, one just explores to see if there is a "fit."

DS: In your opinion, what does it take to become a millionaire?

AA: Dreams (generalized). Goals (specific). Action/Execution (most important thing that far too few people engage in). Persistence. Measurement to monitor progress. "F" for feedback, so one is continuously learning and growing.

DS: What does it take to have a high level of confidence?

AA: Long Term: know and live your values. Identify value conflicts. Know and pursue your dreams like a man on fire. Shorter Term: the Adel triad results in "state" management: physiology, focus, and inner language pattern. Therefore, put yourself into peak physiology through exercise, peak language patterns by watching your inner dialogue and vocabulary, and proactive thinking so you control what you focus upon. What you focus upon expands!

DS: What types of things do you do consistently that keep your confidence level as high as possible?

AA: Exercise, language (incantations), and self-awareness of my confidence levels.

DS: What does the future hold for Adel Anwar?

AA: What it holds for me is what it holds for the world. What amount of value I can add.

DS: How confident are you that you'll get there?

AA: 100 percent.

DS: Is there anything else you'd like to add that readers of this book would be interested to know?

AA: The above interview focused on confidence and memory. Memory was where it started for me. I also became a world expert in another area. It's your "brain component" that is often overlooked yet is the most valuable, most practical, and most useless thing many people do: "think." Most learned people have no idea whatsoever how to think practically. Instead, they are great right/wrong logical thinkers. I show people how to use the mind to think practically and the results of this are the world's most powerful in every area from confidence to memory, and from outstanding wealth to brilliant relationships. My overall expertise is the practical use of the brain.

Chapter Sixteen

CONFIDENCE BLASTS AND KILLERS

We probably wouldn't worry about what people think of us if we could know how seldom they do.

-Olin Miller

The little things make a world of difference in our daily lives. It's been said that if you take care of those little concerns the big items will take care of themselves. The devil really is in the details.

On the following pages, I'll be highlighting some rather simple concepts that can either boost your level of self-esteem or absolutely destroy it. Pay close attention. Make a few subtle changes and it can drastically improve your outlook on the world around you and immediately put a halt to those things you may be doing that are sabotaging your confidence level.

CONFIDENCE BLASTS

- Conceptualize Yourself At Your Best

Perception is reality. Actually visualize how you will look, feel, talk, and act when you are at the top of your game. Keep in mind that if you can't see yourself this way nobody else will either.

- Practice Proactivity

Stop waiting for the other shoe to drop and instead go make things happen. Take jurisdiction over your actions. Launch those great ideas into reality rather than looking back and wondering "what if."

- Strengthen Your Competence Position

Recognize that increased competence can be achieved only through intensified efforts. Rome wasn't built in a day and your competence level won't be either. A consistent and steadfast approach to improvement in the areas that are important to your performance is essential.

- Stick Up For Yourself

Nobody can take advantage of you unless you allow it. The meek shall inherit the earth and that's exactly what you'll be bequeathed until you realize that you have a voice and it needs to be heard. What is it that you fancy, need, or desire? Figure it out and then ask for it!

- Take Baby Steps

It's easy to feel overwhelmed when your goal seems like it's light-years ahead. Instead of putting all of your focus on the result, emphasize what you can do right now to simply take the next step in the process. Keep in mind that the key to yielding long-lasting outcomes is the consistent regularity of small upgrades and advancement.

- Look The Part

Jerry Rice, arguably the greatest wide receiver in National Football League history, used to say that "when you look good—you feel good. And when you feel good—you play good." Ain't that the truth!

Make sure you feel great about your presentation to the world every single day. Are your clothes worn, dated, and out of style? Go get some new ones now! Can't afford them? So what, get them anyway and consider it an investment in your future in the same manner your student loans are.

- Get Motivated And Inspired On A Daily Basis

I always think of the following Zig Ziglar quote whenever I hear people criticize those who seek out daily forms of inspiration because they say it goes away quickly. "People often say that motivation doesn't last. Well, neither does bathing—that's why we recommend it daily."

There are thousands of techniques in order to do this on a consistent basis. Some simple ways are just to read an inspirational blog, listen to your favorite uplifting music, or, if you're a religious person, go ahead and review some of your favorite Bible passages. The key here is for you to do whatever it takes to keep yourself motivated and inspired all of the time.

- Be Conscious Of Your Principles And Behave By Them

In order for your life to feel like it has purpose, you must have values and beliefs that are important to you. Without these ethics and standards, it's very easy to get off track. But with them, your daily decision-making process becomes so much clearer due to the confidence of your conviction. Being guided by those things that are most consequential to you has a way of really providing clarity in reference to your thoughts, words, and deeds.

• Be Genuinely Happy For Others And Celebrate Their Triumphs With Them

Treat everybody on earth the way you would want them to treat your momma. Jealousy is a concept that should be foreign to you as it serves no good purpose. Recognize that people make their own luck through their efforts; let their successes serve as a reminder that it works the exact same way for you too. Plus, you'll need people to party with when you win too!

• Get Up Early And Accomplish Your Most Important Tasks First

So many people procrastinate when it comes to doing the important but not critical activities on their to-do list. It's vital to understand that the longer you put it off the larger the burden grows in your mind. Attack these undertakings early in the day and your feeling of achievement will propel you to get done more than you ever imagined.

• Write It Down!

Putting your intentions, aspirations, and desires on paper is a powerful first step to achieving them. Having these ambitions in a concrete format like this allows you to refer to them often as you move confidently in the direction of your dreams. Not having these targets on paper is akin to trying to throw darts at a bull's-eye while blindfolded.

• Be Warmhearted, Unselfish, And Generous

By giving to others in this manner, you'll actually be giving yourself a more positive self-image as well as increased character.

Knowing deep down that you are truly a good person is one of the best confidence blasts there is. But don't do it because it may help you. Instead, be this way because it's right and decent and the way you should be. Without it, there is no confidence, just possible arrogance.

• Make A Big Decision And Announce It To The World

Let all of your peeps know that you have decided to take action and succeed! This does a number of things to help boost your self-esteem. Just by proclaiming what you're going to do lets you and everyone else know you have a plan. You have also got the added motivation of not wanting to look like someone who talks a good game but never backs it up. And, just as importantly, by announcing your intentions to all those in your life you've just created a large support group of people who care about you and will encourage you to succeed. Don't be shy. Get to that mountaintop and shout out your intentions to the whole planet!

• Break A Sweat!

Physically fit people are generally more confident than those who have allowed themselves to get out of shape over the years. Part of it is self-image but part of it is simply feeling good. It's not easy to have an abundance of self-esteem if you rarely feel at your best physically. A strong workout does wonders before a big presentation or a night out on the town.

• Smile

As mentioned earlier, smiling is the fastest and easiest way known to humankind to immediately become better looking. Not only is it free, but it helps you to feel better about yourself and to be nicer to others. And you better believe that smiling breeds confidence. And having confidence is very attractive.

- Take Everything Serious But Yourself

Your dreams, your work, your to do list. Take all of the above as
serious as a heart attack. It's the only way to achieve. But lighten
up a little on how you take yourself, man! Number one, it's not
very becoming when you run across someone who sees their own
self as the good lord's gift to the human race. Learn to laugh at
yourself when applicable and by all means cut yourself a little
slack when things don't go your way.

- Be Prepared

Nothing instills confidence more than preparation. Just think
back to your school days when you had to take a test. Forgot to
study? Uh oh, not feeling so confident there, huh? But when
you're prepared, I mean really, really prepared, your confidence
level shoots through the roof. You've got to get to the point
where you're no longer going through life "winging it." That just
leads to anxiety, poor performance, and low self-esteem. Over
prepare and you'll knock 'em dead, guaranteed.

- Take Risks

Not with your life, mind you. But take calculated risks that
make life exciting and the potential outcomes rewarding. We've
all heard the saying "without great risk there can be no great
rewards" and boy is that true. Risk takers are a confident bunch.
Join the crew.

- Be Thankful

Ninety-nine percent of all the other human beings on this planet
have it worse off than you. Don't believe me? Do you have a roof
over your head when it's time to go to sleep at night? Do you
have food to eat when you're hungry and clean water to drink

when you're thirsty? I'll bet you even have some new clothes to wear for those special occasions. And do you have any idea how many millions of people in this world don't even have shoes to wear? Yeah, be thankful and show some gratitude for the blessings you have. None of us has ever gotten to where we are today without the help of others, so show them some love too. Give thanks all the time and not just on Thanksgiving and watch what it does to your perception of yourself.

- Give Sincere Compliments Freely

Confident people know how to dish out the compliments. The more specific the better. Be careful not to do it because you're fishing for one in return. It doesn't work that way. You'll come across as a phony. Be as genuine and authentic as possible and the message will be received kindly. And you'll feel even better about yourself.

- Be A Man Or Woman Of Your Word

If you told them you'd be there at three o'clock then be there at three o'clock! Pay your debts on time. Under promise and over deliver. Have your mouth stop this practice of writing checks that you can't cash. Knowing deep down that people can count on you is a great confidence booster.

- Confront Your Anxieties Head On

Nothing makes you feel better about yourself than facing your fears with courage and overcoming them. And there is nothing that stops you from being the person you strive to be more than avoiding those situations you are terrified of. Everybody's scared from time to time. The most confident people I know aren't the best at what they do; they're just the bravest.

• Stop Caring So Much What Others Think

Just like with fear, worrying too much about what people think about you or your actions often has paralyzing effects. Yes it's important to be viewed professionally and positively by your clients, co-workers, and boss. And you absolutely want your family and friends to love you unconditionally and see you in the best light as possible. But please understand this crucial difference. When you're a good person and lead a good life they're going to view you in that regard. So stop worrying what they all think about your clothes, your words, or your actions. Accomplishing anything worthwhile would be virtually impossible if you had to get everybody's approval before taking action. Remember again that what they think about you is really none of your business.

• Develop A Motto

During the recent downturn in the economy, I told my sales team, "We've decided not to participate in the recession." And then we went out and sold millions and millions of dollars above and beyond our goals. That was our slogan, our rallying cry. Nike told the world to "Just Do It" for many years. "Failure is not an option" is a strong one. And I've always felt a sudden dose of American patriotism whenever I'd see a red, white, and blue T-shirt with the saying "These colors don't run." Construct your own phrase, one you can live by. It should be congruent with the prime concerns in your life. Learn it, live it, and love it!

CONFIDENCE KILLERS

• Taking Things Personally

Develop some thicker skin, would 'ya, man? Don't take everything people say or do as a personal affront. It's a good bet that the other person treats everybody that way and it's got nothing to do with you. Sensitivity is an awesome trait to have when it comes to dealing with infants. Not so much though when you find yourself in competitive environments. Learn to just "let it go."

- Believing That Hope Is A Strategy

When my son was just a little boy I used to enjoy watching him throw pennies into the wishing well. He'd say things like "I'm gonna play for the Steelers when I grow up." Or, "I hope to be a fireman someday." Aw, how cute he was. Of course, we all know that wishing and hoping as grown-ups only leads to disappointment and failure. Not exactly the stuff confidence is built upon. I'll take a well thought out blueprint that has been transferred to paper in the form a real plan any day.

- Constant Complaining

Shut up already! How can you possibly feel great about yourself when you're endlessly finding fault and kvetching about everybody and everything? Trust me, it's impossible. Start to look for the good in the whole kit and caboodle, and then focus on that. There's enough real negativity all around us that we certainly don't need to always call attention to it.

- Worry And Fear

Think about the worst possible thing that can happen. And then what if it really does happen? OK, now answer yourself this. How did all that worry and fear help? It didn't so knock it off. It's paralyzing, remember. And being rendered immobile is no way to move confidently in the direction of your dreams.

- Disorganization

Living and/or working in a chaotic and clutter-filled environment is a surefire way to knock your self-esteem down a few rungs. We've also seen the reality shows where the house is so messy they don't want any guests for fear of what they might think. Maybe that's the way your office or cubicle looks right now. And you don't live in your car so why does it look like you do? Clean up your surroundings and develop systems for where things go and you'll immediately begin to feel better about yourself.

• Hanging Out With Negative People

You will begin to act like those you spend the most time with so be very careful who those people are. It's been said that misery loves company and this group could sell out every stadium in the world. The only entrance requirement to this club is a bad attitude. I'd rather not belong to an organization that is so easy to get into.

• Comparing And Competing

In the real world, you have to compete very hard to be successful. That's not what I'm talking about here. I'm referring to those who are always trying to "keep up with the Joneses." She got a new purse so you have to get a new purse. Your kid plays basketball? So does mine and he's a starter on the fifth grade team! The constant need to be relevant and make yourself feel as though you belong is a drain on your belief system. It's unnecessary, and frankly, a bore.

• Being A Wuss

Not having a backbone is a surefire way to lack confidence. These people let everybody else dictate to them. They'll manipulate your time, thoughts, words, and money if you let them. And if you're a namby-pamby softie, you probably do.

• Depending Too Much On Others

Listen. If the outcome you desire often rests with the actions of someone else, you've got a problem. Wean yourself off the baby bottle and take responsibility for your own success or failure. Confident people love the way they get to control their own destiny. You are the only person who can guarantee that you won't be let down by relying on someone else for a positive outcome.

- Treating Your Body Like A Garbage Disposal

It's not possible to be the most confident you imaginable when you're feeding your body junk and lying on the couch all day. It's never too late to reverse a trend and now would be a great time to begin to alter this one.

Chapter Seventeen

CONCLUSION

When there is no enemy within, the enemies outside cannot hurt you.

-African Proverb

Having a high level of self-confidence is a choice that you absolutely must consciously make. Leaving your self-esteem and belief system up to chance is a gamble that most people cannot afford to take. The consequences are usually too great. I'm talking about repercussions like underemployment, infrequent and poor personal relationships, and worst of all, unhappiness. Life is way too short for that nonsense if you ask me. The moment you decide it's time to get about the business of building a better you is the exact instant it will all start to change for the better.

Look around. The happiest people in the world are the ones who feel great about themselves. They come in all shapes, colors, and sizes. Their common bond is that they all possess a great attitude. It's not what happens to them that matters most but how they react to it. Because that's what confident people do. Victims, on the other hand, always wonder (usually out loud) why all these bad things keep happening to them.

Confident people always think they "can." That's more than half the battle. Having low self-esteem and not believing in your own abilities is a nonstarter. An appropriate analogy is trying to go rock climbing with one hand tied behind your back. It's damn near impossible. And most people wouldn't even try to climb that rock under those circumstances just as the majority of folks who lack confidence rarely try anything new if it requires bold action on their part. They just run in quicksand all the time when they should be jumping right over it.

Confident people **do**. Constant action is their signature. Even if they fall short of a goal, other opportunities and outcomes often manifest due to their high activity levels. An object in motion stays in motion.

All people on this earth have different confidence levels when it comes to the myriad of challenges they face in their daily lives. Some people were fortunate enough to be born into the type of confidence-nurturing environment that has made it easier for them to feel great about who they are. But, as we talked about earlier, confidence can be and is learned.

There is a common thread among all people, however. We all get to choose whether to recognize that our belief systems are a living organism that needs exercise in order to strengthen, grow, and solidify. Of course, just recognizing this fact is one thing. Acting on it is something entirely different.

Understand and utilize the **FOUR STEPS TO A MORE CONFIDENT YOU** that I've laid out in this book. Keep in mind that the system is foundational. Each step builds on the previous one. I truly believe that it's inconceivable not to raise your confidence level to heights you've never known as long as you follow this simple path.

So often in life our failures are the result of us just not doing what we know we have to in order to succeed. The obese guy who won't stop eating, the poor student who won't study, the unemployed gal who won't look for a job.

But it's not just the obvious situations like above that scream out for action. How about the CEO who doesn't have the courage to produce real change? Or the doctor who lacks the conviction to not let her patients manipulate the diagnosis and the treatment? Or the coach who can't transfer a winning attitude to his players?

Confidence, and a lack thereof, touches everything you do. Raise yours exponentially and watch your entire universe improve.

Let's review the **FOUR STEPS TO A MORE CONFIDENT YOU**:

STEP #1

THE MIND, BODY, AND SOUL
CONFIDENCE FOUNDATION PYRAMID

1. Build and grow this nucleus with great care.

2. Your MIND is a muscle that needs to work out daily. Feed it a steady diet of new information that relates to your craft as well as current events. Have outside interests. Schedule this time wisely, as it's the gasoline a confident brain needs to run on.

3. Respect your BODY and treat it like the place where you live. Get that heart rate going as often as possible. Keep those muscles strong. Don't be a garbage disposal and eat like it's the Last Supper every meal. Be wary of destructive physical activities like smoking and drugs. You can't feel great about yourself if you don't feel great. Period.

4. Have an honest conversation with yourself and dig down deep into your SOUL. Answer the questions that will serve as your driving forces on a daily basis. Who are you? What motivates you to get up in the morning, go out in this rough but wonderful world, and give it your all? What do you want out of life for you and your family? What do you have faith in? And most significantly, what is the most important thing in the world to you?

STEP #2

YOUR POSSE OF INSPIRATION

1. Recognize that there are people right now in your circle of influence that don't necessarily have the most positive effect on you and often sway your thinking in the wrong direction. Family members and co-workers often fall into this category.

2. Develop your own POSSE OF INSPIRATION in order to have a group of constructive, successful, and progressive people who will enlighten, encourage, and promote you and your agenda.

3. Keep in mind that your POSSE is a fluid group that may change with some degree of frequency.

STEP #3

HAVE NO FEAR—DEVELOP COURAGE

1. It's a known fact that fear paralyzes one from taking action. Just realizing this is the first step to overcome it.

2. Ask yourself what is the worst possible thing that can happen if you act. Because if you don't, nothing will happen. And that's bad.

3. When truly petrified act "as if" and "fake it until you make it."

4. Learn to train your mind to fast-forward to a better place automatically when debilitating fear sets in.

STEP #4

UNDERSTANDING THE ACTIONS-RESULTS-BELIEFS CIRCLE

1. ACTIONS come before RESULTS in the dictionary and in real life. You must act when your head knows you should even though the rest of you is resisting.

2. The RESULTS will come. The question is how fast? And that's entirely up to you.

3. Your eventual RESULTS will undoubtedly translate into deep-rooted BELIEFS.

4. The BELIEFS you hold are at the core of who you are. Believe in you and look out world!

Watch any sporting event at the highest level and you'll notice a few things that relate to confidence. The difference in talent between the participants is usually very small, sometimes even microscopic. Often the eventual winner is the champion who has more belief in his or her abilities and the outcome than the other person and has literally willed him or herself to victory. Reality mirrors that exactly.

Treat people with equal amounts of respect regardless of their position in life and how much money they make. It's called karma and it's the way all decent human beings should act. There is nobody below you or above you in the grand scheme of things. People with world-class confidence make everybody else they encounter feel great. Smile and the whole world smiles back at you.

Understand the distinction between confidence and arrogance. Others rarely come away from an encounter with an egotistical self-important person feeling good about them or you. Deep down, these types of individuals are actually insecure and they are masking their fears with overbearing pompousness. Don't be one of them.

Learn from everybody but especially those who have overcome to achieve some level of greatness. Nothing builds confidence more than hurdling obstacles. Adversity is one hell of a teacher and the wisest among us study them so they won't repeat the mistakes of others. Seek out people who have been where you want to go and learn their stories. Take the best they have to offer and leave the rest. Mostly, model their success activities and discover from their trials and tribulations what to avoid.

The coolest people I've ever met are also the most authentic and confident. Learn from others but don't act like them. Always strive to be a first rate version of yourself rather than a second rate version of someone else. We all know that copies are never as good as the original.

The beauty of confidence is that once you've got it the whole picture becomes clearer and easier. Everything is more attracted to you. Respect, friendships, the opposite sex, money, etc. It's not always easy to obtain but what worthwhile thing is? Work at it and live the life you deserve. You're the only one holding you back.

Rare Confidence. Get some.

ABOUT THE AUTHOR

One of the most passionate and inspirational leaders you'll ever meet, David Shirey is a tremendously accomplished executive with a successful record in national sales management, team building, introducing new products to market, and media relations while dealing in extremely competitive and technical markets.

He is a true hands-on leader who has a proven history of immediate and dramatic impact—utilizing a genuine, upbeat, and infectious leadership style.

David spent over five years directing all sales activities for the largest of Lamar Advertising's 165 markets while spending time each week leading confidence building and sales training sessions. David's team exceeded company-set budgets twenty out of his last twenty-one months in this role during one of the worst economies in modern American history. Producing $32M of revenue in 2010, which was 16 percent over their $27M budget, David's motto was "We've decided not to participate in this recession!"

Spending the early part of the last decade as the director of sports sales for IRIS Technologies' Landro Play Analyzer Division, David led all sales and business development activities of this extraordinary technology to the sports world. David's group increased sales over 200 percent three straight years while he was front and center with the media touting this incredible coaching tool.

During the mid and late 1990s, David worked as director of the New Business Development Division of Computer Enterprises, Inc., guiding sales operations for this IT services firm. David oversaw offices in Pittsburgh, New York, and Los Angeles while helping the organization to receive a very high ranking on the Inc. Magazine list of America's fastest growing, privately held companies.

David has been involved with and/or supported dozens of charities in recent years including: Coaches vs. Cancer, March of Dimes, the Jewish Community Center of Pittsburgh, the Lymphoma & Leukemia Society, the Muscular Dystrophy Association, the Carnegie Mellon University School of Art, and Autism Speaks.

David holds a bachelor's degree from Ohio University and manages multiple youth baseball teams in the Pittsburgh area where he resides with his wife, Lisa; son, Alex; and dog, Lacy.

For more information on how David may be able to help you or your business go to www.davidshirey.com.

Printed in Germany
by Amazon Distribution
GmbH, Leipzig